MIXELLANY'S

# BARIANA

## THE COLLECTOR'S EDITION

Includes

The original 1896 French edition by Louis Fouquet

plus

Mixellany's Annotated Bariana:
A Practical Compendium of
All American and British drinks

translated and annotated by
Charles Vexenat

MIXELLANY

MIXELLANY LIMITED

Mixellany books may be purchased for educational, business, or sales promotional use. For information, please write to Mixellany Limited, 13 Bonchurch Road, West Ealing, London W13 9JE United Kingdom or email jared@mixellany.com

First edition

ISBN 13: 978-1-907434-02-0

British Library Cataloguing in Publication Data.
A catalogue record for this book is available from the British Library.

# CONTENTS

# PUBLISHER'S NOTE

Throughout this translation of *Bariana: Recueil pratique de toutes boissons Americaines et Anglaise* we have typeset Charles Vexenat's annotations in a different typeface than the main text to make it easier to read his commentaries.

# PREFACE

Originally published in 1896, *Bariana: Recueil pratique de toutes boissons Americaines et Anglaises* by Louis Fouquet is regarded as the second French cocktail book ever published. The first French cocktail book appeared in 1889, titled *Methode pour composer soi même les boissons Americaines, Anglaises, Italiennes, etc.*, compiling 250 formulas for use by "*limonadiers*, restaurateurs, maitres d'hôtel, chefs de buffets, chefs de bars, maisons bourgeoises, etc."

The 109-page booklet was put together by Emile Leveuvre, Chef de Bar of the Cosmopolite in Paris, who wanted to help the French bar industry to host foreign visitors in the proper way by delivering the mixed drink these patrons were used to like cocktails, collins, sours, daisies, cobblers, and punches.

Interestingly—and out of nowhere—Emile Leveuvre listed "wodka" as a Russian eau-de-vie but unfortunately he does not list any mixed drinks with this liquor.

There is no question that *Bariana* is the first heralded French cocktail book; it was unveiled in the popular *Almanach Hachette* encyclopaedia on practical life and introduced the phenomenon of a nouveau genre of mixed drinks.

Published annually from 1894 to 1992, the almanac was a classic miscellany of information: French economy, French education, French history, French law, French politics, French society and medicine, sports, gardening, technology, and world history amongst other useful quotidian life tips.

The 1898 edition's calendar included a handful of American and English beverage recipes excerpted from *Bariana*. The month of November suggested winter drinks and cocktails. Summer drinks, juleps, cobblers and punches appeared in August. May introduced some miscellaneous drinks and the personage:

> "These sophisticated and stimulating drinks, although made for the American palate, are becoming more and more fashionable in Europe. Up to the present day their recipes had remained the specialty of foreign bars, and outside these, we ignored the manners on how to prepare cocktails and cobblers.

> "Thanks to Mr. Louis Fouquet, the skilful barman from the Criterion (121 r. St-Lazare) American and English beverages can now be prepared by everyone as easily as combining anisette and water.

> "From this volume that he has just published under the title *Bariana* (Price: 2 francs) we chose for the readers of the almanac, the following recipes..."

Their careful seasonal selection is the confirmation that drinks of the era were tied to the harvests and specific to a purpose: beverages tempering the summer heat and curing the chills of winter, spring and fall were just pure joy! The recipes included in *Almanach Hachette* are:

Ale Flip
Blue Blazer
Brandy and Honey
Brandy Cobbler
Champagne Julep
Criterion's Own Punch
Eye Opener
Gin Sling (chaud)
Japanese Cocktail
Last Drink
Magnolia
Martinian Vermouth Cocktail
Milk Punch
Morning Call
Mother Milk
Queen Charlotte
Sam Ward
Sleeper
Special Coffee Cocktail
Thunder
Victoria Cocktail

I could not dig up much information about the original Criterion in Paris. It closed long ago. And the man himself? He was a certainly barman and a *limonadier*: an old French term for someone making and selling lemonade but generalising to bar, bistro, coffee shop owners selling more beverages than food. Working at The Criterion rue St-Lazare, Fouquet would have been serving artists, painters, illustrators and other avant-garde bohemians who lived in the Montmartre district such as Henri de Toulouse Lautrec, as they drowned themselves in absinthe and other beverages.

In 1899, this enthusiastic man opened his own a small hideout on a residential corner of the Champs-Élysées and the avenue Georges V, behind door number 99: The Criterion-Fouquet's Bar. Soon the bistro became the hangout for horse carriage drivers, coachmen and maids working in the area.

At the turn of the 20th century, all things London became fashionable in Paris and Louis decided follow the movement. The name of the bistro was too much of a mouthful for the regular patrons. So, around 1903 he decided to shorten his venue's name to "Fouquet's" keeping the 's' to gain popularity with the Anglo-Saxon community. It was an instant success, and carried on after his death in 1905 from typhoid fever.

This "Brasserie Parisienne" is still open, and to the present day is one of the most famous in Paris. I went there to find out more, told the receptionist I was writing an "article" and explained that I was looking for information about it and the founder and the place. She smiled and handed me the generic tourist brochure detailing more glamorous red carpet parties and celebrities per square meter in the last hundred years than almost any other French establishment, but nothing of the true birth of the place and its cocktails.

I dragged myself to the bar to take a peek at the menu. I recognised the head bartender: I had worked with him briefly in

Louis FOUQUET Propriétaire

# FOUQUET'S BAR

## The Criterion

### ENGLISH & AMERICAN BAR

## GRILL ROOM

| APÉRITIFS Français....... | Le verre, 0ʳ50 - Gᵈ verre, 0ʳ60 |
| ABSINTHES de Marques. | Le verre, 0ʳ60 - Gᵈ verre, 0ʳ75 |
| LIQUEURS CUSENIER Supérieures.. | Le verre, 0ʳ75 - Sirops, 0ʳ60 |

## LA MAISON N'A PAS DE SUCCURSALE

### GRANDE SPÉCIALITÉ D'HUITRES FINES

Du 1ᵉʳ Octobre au 15 Avril

ÉTABLISSEMENT OUVERT jusqu'à 2 h. du matin

PRIX DES HUITRES :

| | La douz. | La cent |
|---|---|---|
| Marennes vertes extra | 3 » | 22 » |
| supérieures | 2 50 | 18 » |
| 1ᵉʳ choix | 2 » | 16 » |
| moyennes | 1 50 | 11 » |
| blanches extra | 2 » | 15 » |
| 1ᵉʳ choix | 1 50 | 11 » |
| Cancales extra | 3 » | 22 » |
| supérieures | 2 50 | 18 » |
| 1ʳᵉ choix | 2 » | 15 » |
| Armoricaines de Belon | 3 » | 22 » |
| supérieures | 1 75 | 13 » |
| Ostendes Victoria | 3 » | 22 » |
| 1ᵉʳ choix | 2 50 | 18 » |
| Natives de Zélande | 4 » | 30 » |
| d'Angleterre | 3 » | 22 » |
| Côtes Rouges impériales | 6 » | 45 » |
| Royal Whistable | 5 » | 36 » |
| Colchester | 5 » | 30 » |
| Burnham | » 90 | 6 50 |
| Portugaises extra | » 70 | 5 » |
| choisies | | |

### ESCARGOTS DE BOURGOGNE

OUVERTURE A DOMICILE

Expédition en France et à l'Etranger

LES COMMANDES SONT REÇUES JUSQU'A 2 H. DU MATIN

Téléphone 814-02

| Saumon fumé | le kilo, 12 » |
| Sproots de Hollande | » 75 la douzaine |
| Anguilles fumées, Haddocks, Kippers, etc. | |

BARIANA

RECUEIL COMPLET

POUR FAIRE SOI-MÊME LES BOISSONS AMÉRICAINES

En vente ici. — Prix : 2 francs

### GRAND Sᵗ-LOUIS LIQVOR

Liqueur digestive à base de vieille fine Champagne

La Bouteille : 5 francs

La plus grande Maison de Vins de tout Paris

### GRANDE FACTORERIE VINICOLE DE FRANCE

133, Rue Montmartre. — Demandez le Catalogue

### E. BRUYER & ses Fils

CHAUFFAGE - ALIMENTATION

SIÈGE SOCIAL :

2, Rue Saint-Denis, PARIS (1ᵉʳ) Châtelet

TÉLÉPHONE 106-43

USINES ET ENTREPOTS :

62, Quai d'Yvry & Rue Galilée, IVRY-PORT (Seine)

TÉLÉPHONE 801-95

Thé du Criterion .............. 20 fr. le kilo

(Fouquet's Bar menu courtesy of Mauro Majoub and Brian Rea.)

**s les parcs et ne passe par aucun intermédiaire**

# WINE LIST

## VINS DE CHAMPAGNE

| | Bouteille | 1/2 Bout |
|---|---|---|
| Clicquot grand vin brut | 18 » | » |
| Ayala, extra dry | 16 » | 8 50 |
| Perrier et Jouet, brut | 16 » | 8 50 |
| Pommery-Greno, extra sec | 16 » | 8 50 |
| Pommery-Greno (sec, Drapeau améri- | | |
| cain) | 16 · | 8 50 |
| Louis Roederer, grand vin sec | 16 » | 8 50 |
| G.-H. Mumm, cordon rouge | 16 » | 8 50 |
| Saint-Marceaux very dry et brut | 16 » | 8 50 |
| Heidsieck, dry monopole | 16 » | 8 50 |
| Bollinger brut | 16 » | 8 50 |
| **JULES MUMM**, extra dry | 16 » | 8 50 |
| Irroy brut | 16 » | 8 50 |
| Montebello, maximum sec | 16 » | 8 50 |
| Montebello, cordon noir | 12 » | 6 50 |
| Moët et Chandon, carte bleue | 10 » | 5 50 |
| Criterion, réserve, sec | 6 » | 3 50 |
| Louis XV (tisane) | 5 » | 2 75 |
| Pol Roger brut 1893 | 18 » | » |

### CHAMPAGNE HENRIOT

| | | |
|---|---|---|
| Sillery, 1re qualité (doux) | 6 50 | 3 75 |
| Sillery, supérieur (doux) | 7 50 | 4 » |
| Dry carte blanche (demi-sec) | 9 50 | 5 » |
| Silver Label (sec) | 9 50 | 5 » |

### EAUX MINÉRALES

| | | |
|---|---|---|
| Saint-Galmier | 0 75 | 0 50 |
| Appolinaris | 1 50 | 1 » |
| Evian | 1 50 | 0 75 |
| Vichy Célestins | 1 25 | 0 75 |
| Vals | 1 25 | » |
| Siphons | 0 50 | » |

### SCHWEPPE'S WATERS

| | | |
|---|---|---|
| Sodas | 0 60 | 0 40 |
| Ginger Ale | 0 60 | » |
| Ginger Beer | 0 60 | » |
| Lemonade | 0 60 | » |
| Seltzer | 0 60 | » |

## VINS DE BORDEAUX

### ROUGES

| | Bouteille | 1/2 Bout |
|---|---|---|
| Fronsac | 1 50 | 1 » |
| Ludon | 2 » | 1 25 |
| Saint-Émilion 1893 | 2 50 | » |
| Margaux | 3 » | 1 75 |
| Saint-Émilion | 4 » | « |
| Saint-Julien | 5 » | » |
| Ch. Pontet Canet | 6 » | » |
| Batailley | 7 » | » |

### BLANCS

| | | |
|---|---|---|
| Podensac | 1 50 | 1 » |
| Barsac | 2 » | 1 25 |
| **LA BRÈDE, Bordeaux blanc SEC** | 2 50 | « |
| Preignac | 3 » | 1 75 |
| Haut-Sauternes | 4 » | » |
| Château Lamothe | 5 » | » |
| Vedrines | 6 » | » |
| Sudulraut | 7 » | » |
| Château-Yquem (authentique) | 10 » | » |

## VINS DE BOURGOGNE

### ROUGES

| | | |
|---|---|---|
| Mâcon | 1 50 | 1 » |
| Thorins | 2 » | 1 25 |
| Volnay | 4 » | 2 25 |
| Beaune Hospice | 6 » | » |
| Pomard | 6 » | 3 25 |

### BLANCS

| | | |
|---|---|---|
| Chablis | 2 » | 1 25 |
| Clos de la Chaume | 4 » | » |
| Vouvray | 2 » | 1 25 |
| Saumur | 2 » | 1 25 |
| Saumur 1895 | 3 » | » |
| Pouilly | 4 » | 2 25 |
| Montrachet | 7 » | 3 75 |

### VIN DU RHIN

| | | |
|---|---|---|
| Laubeinheimer | 3 » | » |
| Winninger (Moselle) | 3 » | » |

### " ALLSOPP'S "

**Pale Ale, Stout, Lager Beer (ON DRAUGHT)**

| | | | |
|---|---|---|---|
| La Pinte | 0.80 | La 1/2 Bouteille | 0.75 |
| La 1/2 Pinte | 0.40 | Le Bock | 0.40 |
| La Bouteille | 1.50 | Le Double | 0.60 |

Ces Bières sont vendues 1 franc le litre par 6 litres
(verre non compris)

# AMERICAN AND ENGLISH DRINKS

## COCKTAILS

| | | |
|---|---|---|
| Vermouth | 0 | 75 |
| Gin | » | 75 |
| Sherry | 0 | 75 |
| Brandy | » | 75 |
| Whisky | » | 75 |
| Absinthe | » | 75 |
| Martini | » | 75 |
| Mannhattan | 1 | » |
| Rye Whisky | 1 | » |
| Bourbon Whisky | 1 | » |
| Champagne | 1 | » |

*(COCKTAILS)*

## SHORT DRINKS

| | | |
|---|---|---|
| Prairie Oyster | 1 | » |
| Square Meal | 1 | » |
| Egg. Flip | 1 | » |
| Whiskey Sour | 1 | » |
| Pick-me-up | 1 | » |
| Pousse-l'Amour | 1 | » |
| Corpse Reviver | 1 | » |
| Knickebein | 1 | » |
| Pousse-Café | 1 | » |
| Gin Sour | 1 | » |
| Sherry-Flip. — Port Flip | 1 | » |
| Last Drink | 1 | » |

## SUMMER DRINKS (ICED)
### BOISSONS GLACÉES

| | | |
|---|---|---|
| Lemon Squash | « | 75 |
| Orangeade | » | 75 |
| Orgeat Lemonade | 1 | » |
| Mint Julep (à la Menthe fraîche | 1 | » |
| Strawberry punch | 1 | » |
| American Lemonade | 1 | » |
| John Collins | 1 | » |
| Gin Fizz | 1 | » |
| Brandy Sling | 1 | » |

## WINTER DRINKS (HOT)
### BOISSONS CHAUDIS

| | | |
|---|---|---|
| American grog | » | 75 |
| Port Negus | » | 75 |
| Milk Punch | 1 | » |
| Tom and Jerry | 1 | » |
| Gin Toddy | » | 75 |
| Whiskey Toddy | » | 75 |
| Rhum Punch | » | 75 |
| Brandy Punch | » | 75 |
| Groog ordinaire | » | 60 |

## LONG DRINKS
### BOISSONS GLACÉES

| | | |
|---|---|---|
| Ice Cream Soda | 1 | » |
| Soyer au Champagne | 1 | » |
| Port Sangaree | 1 | » |
| Egg Nogg | 1 | » |
| Soda Cocktail | 1 | » |
| Champagne Cup | 1 | » |
| Brandy Smash | 1 | » |
| Claret Cup | 1 | » |
| Ided Coffee | 1 | » |
| Chicago | 1 | » |

## COBBLERS ET PUNCHS
### BOISSONS GLACÉES

| | | |
|---|---|---|
| Gin and Milk | 1 | » |
| Milk Punch | 1 | » |
| Claret Punch | 1 | » |
| Brandy Punch | 1 | » |
| Sherry Cobbler | 1 | » |
| Brandy Cobbler | 1 | » |
| Champagne Cobbler | 1 | » |
| Vanilla Punch | 1 | » |
| Gin Punch | 1 | » |

## STRAIGHT DRINKS

| | | |
|---|---|---|
| Champagne sec ou doux. le verre | 1 | » |
| Fraise Champagne la flûte | » | 75 |
| Exportation Bock | » | 50 |
| Amer champagne | » | 75 |

## GIN-WHISKIES, ETC.

| | Plate | Avec 1/2 soda | Le Soda | la bout |
|---|---|---|---|---|
| Scotch Whisky | » 75 | 1 » | 1 25 | 4 » |
| Irish Whisky | » 75 | 1 » | 1 25 | 4 » |
| Rye Whisky | » 75 | 1 » | 1 25 | 7 50 |
| Bourbon | » 75 | 1 » | 1 25 | 7 50 |
| Brandy | » 75 | 1 » | 1 25 | 7 50 |
| Gin (Plymouth) | » 75 | 1 » | 1 25 | 7 50 |
| Schiedam | » 75 | 1 » | 1 25 | 25 |
| John Dewar | » 75 | 1 » | 1 25 | 6 50 |
| Dewar liqueur | » 75 | 1 » | 1 25 | 7 50 |
| John Walker | » 75 | 1 » | 1 25 | 6 50 |
| John Jameson | » 75 | 1 » | 1 25 | 6 50 |
| Canadian Club | » 75 | 1 » | 1 25 | 7 50 |
| My old Scotch | » 75 | 1 - | 1 25 | 12 |
| Hunter-Rye | » 75 | 1 » | 1 25 | 7 50 |
| Guckenhelmer | » 75 | » 1 | 1 25 | 7 50 |

## Vins d'Espagne et de Portugal
### SANDEMAN & Cⁱᵉ

### PORTO ROUGE & BLANC
le verre la bout.

| | | | |
|---|---|---|---|
| A. Good | » | 3 25 | |
| B. Superior sec Imperial | » 75 | 4 25 | |
| C. Very superior | 1 » | 6 25 | |

### SHERRY OU XÉRÉS

| | | | |
|---|---|---|---|
| A. Good | » | 3 25 | |
| B. Seco Imperial | » 75 | 4 25 | |
| C. Solera | 1 » | 6 25 | |

### MALAGA ROUGE

| | | | |
|---|---|---|---|
| A | » | 3 25 | |
| B. Sec | » 75 | 4 25 | |
| C | 1 » | 6 25 | |

### MADÈRE DE L'ILE

| | | | |
|---|---|---|---|
| A. Good | » | 3 25 | |
| B. Very old Imperial | » 75 | 4 25 | |
| C. Fine | 1 » | 6 25 | |
| Marsala | » 75 | 4 25 | |
| Muscat | » 75 | 4 95 | |
| Banyuls vieux | » 50 | 3 25 | |

*Les prix par bouteilles des Vins d'Espagne sont pour la vente en ville; à consommer ici, il est fait une augmentation de 1 fr. par bouteille.*

| | | |
|---|---|---|
| Thé complet | 1 » | |
| Chocolat complet | 1 » | |
| Café au lait complet | 1 » | |
| Camomille | » 75 | |
| Tilleul | » 75 | |
| Bavaroise | » 75 | |

### SANDWICHES

| | | |
|---|---|---|
| Foie gras | » 50 | |
| Anchois | » 50 | |
| Jambon | » 50 | |
| Chester | » 50 | |
| Roast Beef | 1 » | |
| Langue | » 75 | |

London. I explained the real purpose of my visit and about *Bariana*. To my shock no one there was familiar with the book.

This should not have been too surprising. *Bariana* was published before Louis Fouquet opened his own joint. It was my honour to reintroduce them to an important part of their heritage. And the rest is history.

## ANNOTATIONS ON THE INGREDIENTS

Louis' favourite ingredients in this book are curaçao and crème de noyaux. Both of these liqueurs are used in his original signature drinks as well as some of his personal takes on classic recipes—and he especially loved to mix them together.

Spirits in his time were not as refined as they are today. I believe he was using those liqueurs, in small amounts, to disguise the harsh edges and bad aftertaste of unpleasant liquors.

Louis' mixture works beautifully, curaçao is a tingly bittersweet orange flavour and was often made with rum or cognac at the time adding warmth, body and complexity to his drinks. Louis doesn't mention any particular brand, colour or quality; but I strongly suggest using a high quality 40% ABV style of orange curaçao as the essence will stand up in the drinks better than sticky lower proof ones.

Crème de noyaux comes in two styles: amber and clear. It is produced from dried apricot kernels (*noyaux* is French for fruit pits) macerated then distilled with cognac or Armagnac depending of the style wanted with addition of spices and flower waters. This is often confused with crème de noix, a rich whole nuts liqueur.

It is not surprising Louis used this fragrant liqueur in abundance. Around the mid-1800s, a distillery located in Poissy, a western suburb of Paris was producing the stuff and was highly rated for their quality. Even though there is no guidance in the book on which brand to use, I figured Louis was supporting the local produce.

To test the recipes in *Bariana*, I used the clear Noyau de Poissy, a very delicate 40% ABV liqueur with soft nut flavour, light orange flower nose and some spice fragrances, which sat very well on the back palate in the drinks.

A popular French custom in the late 1800s was to ship rhum agricoles from colonies such as Martinique and Guadeloupe to the main port of Bordeaux where they were aged, blended and bottled on the main land.

Those rhums gained in popularity at the time, and after trying a few different styles for the book, unless specified, it appeared that Rhum agricoles are better to re-create those drinks as they have more sugary pungency from the distilled sugar cane juice. I used a medium aged one for versatility and smoothness.

When it comes to the numerous cognac drinks in the book, Louis is very specific on using Curlier cognac. Curlier has never been a Cognac brand, but there were two Curlier brothers who were Cognac merchants in Jarnac before taking over the management of Courvoisier cognac when their uncle Felix Courvoisier passed away in 1866. Louis was basically buying the aged eau-de-vie from the Curlier brothers and it was probably the stuff made at the distillery they were managing.

On that basis this is the brand I used all the way for the book, and it work really well.

The Dewar's Scotch advert guided me on what whisky style— blended or single malt—to use in the book. Also, remember Phylloxera struck Europe in 1862; single malt was too powerful for most of the population who were used to drinking refined cognac.

Blended whisky placed itself very well as an alternative for many years and gained popularity.

For the Irish whiskey option, I went for the world's most available, Jameson, to make it easy for everyone.

There are a few bourbon libations, I tried them with rye and wheat bourbon. The rye was more my liking, but there is nothing wrong with using a wheated one for softer nuances.

The gin used by Fouquet is not a classic London dry, but a rounder gin not to be confused with Old Tom which is also listed in the book and nowadays reappearing on the market.

The old gin referred to in the recipes is a genever from Holland or maybe a genièvre as it was made in the north of France and Belgium, often aged at the time, with some malty and highly aromatic flavours.

(See the gins and whiskies list from the original 1902 menu on page 12.)

The highly-recommended Sandeman Port and Sherry have been produced since 1790 and are still available nowadays.

Louis also used a lot of powdered sugar to sweeten his drinks. I went for caster sugar as it dissolved better than granulated. Superfine works even better. Please note: Powdered sugar appears in recipes throughout *Bariana*. This is a literal translation but means superfine sugar not confectioner's or icing sugar, which contains cream of tartar or other anti-caking agents and should not be used in a mixed drink.

Flavoured syrups such as raspberry and pineapple, popular at the time, would have been home made as refrigeration wasn't as accurate as it is now, and modern chemical preservatives were unheard of. Fresh fruits cooked in sugar preserved just fine.

Lots of brands are making these flavours nowadays but they can often be of low quality and retain a rather chemical taste. Home made is still the best alternative.

For coffee drinks I used 3 barspoons of instant coffee and in a cup of water as a batch. The coffee at the time wasn't of the best quality so instant is working pretty much in that direction. I am sure espresso coffee lengthened with water could do the trick as well.

Eggs at the time were smaller than now, so I recommend medium or large eggs. When used in a shaken drink I would suggest adding them last as the egg will start to cook and curdle as soon as it contacts the alcohol.

Turin vermouth refers to the sweet Italian style. I used Carpano Antica because I couldn't go wrong with it. There was a sweet French vermouth branded Turin (made by J.M. Turin of Limoges) that I saw in the Exposition Universelle des Vin et Spiritueux collection on Île de Bendor, but I cannot say if Louis was referring to it or the Italian home of vermouth.

## ANNOTATIONS ON THE MEASUREMENT USE IN BARIANA:

It was important to me to stick to Louis' precise measurements and translate them as accurately as possible. To preserve them for everyone as they were originally intended, I found that I had to convert them into millilitres to get a consistency from one to another.

Dashes and drops can mean lots of things. They should be poured from decanters with dasher tops as Louis suggests it. Of course the dasher top can vary from one brand to another and from one bartender to another. I established a standard from an Angostura dasher, and it worked pretty well. For other measures I calculated:

1 spoon = 1 coffee spoon = 1 barspoon = 5 ml
The barspoon drawn on page 26 is the one. Using a classic
Bonzer spoon will work as well as long as it is heaping.

1 small spoon is equal to a barspoon,
which is flat filled to the rim.
1 mouth spoon = 2 barspoons = 10 ml

1 liqueur glass = 30 ml

1 Madeira glass = 60 ml

The term "fill up", varies from what type of glass is used to make
the drink, and from the quantity of ingredients previously poured
into it.

❧

Thanks to Jared and Anistatia for giving me the opportunity to
translate this book and for all their editorial work, Simon Difford and
his team for letting me into the Cabinet Room for several days to test
the drinks, Brian Rea and Greg Boehm for sharing information from
their large book collections and Joseph Biolatto, head bartender of
Bar Le Forum in Paris for sourcing the crème de noyaux for me.

*Et voilà, merci.*

—Charles Vexenat

# INTRODUCTION

In the entire world, there is no country other than America where such a drinks variety exists. Their preparations are so little known by us and so badly mixed by some professional bartenders, all those delicious mixtures are completely neglected by people who like drinks in favour of more harmful and unhealthy aperitifs.

After a few years of experience, I'm happy today to be able to provide to my readers a complete collection allowing them to make very difficult beverages in the blink of an eye just like the most famous American bartenders.

A *limonadier* will be able to make any drink according to the customers' desire. A *maître d'hôtel* will prepare a good cocktail before a delicious diner and embarrassed housewives will be able to offer visiting friends some safely made, refreshing beverages.

Men will find the necessary stimulant from their usage, women delicious and healthy freshness, and the children the gentle flavours of which they are fond.

Pour servir un Cocktail

I have divided my book into six distinct parts:

1°   Cocktails, apéritif drinks;

2°   Short drinks, beverages generally prepared straight into medium size glasses and can be consumed at any time of the day as an imaginative drink;

3°   Cobblers and punches, iced drinks generally garnished with fruits, recommended in hot weather;

4°   Summer Drinks, only to be used during the summer fruit season;

5°   Winter drinks, hot and cheerful;

6°   Punches, for social gatherings, with the necessary quantities for an established number of people.

To make them simpler, every recipe has a reference number for the index and a reference letter corresponding to a glass from the glassware chart that we will consult to use the necessary size glass and the mixing container we will use.

I selected all the barware and glassware mentioned in this book and I put myself at the disposal of anyone who desires to get some in a short time, as I have a supply, shipped from America to satisfy my readers.

—Louis Fouquet

## GLASSES TO USE AND THEIR CAPACITY

A – Mixing glass; Water Capacity: 500 grams
B – Cobbler glass, red and white; Water Capacity: 250 grams
C – Goblet, white, red and green; Water Capacity: 125 grams
D – Cocktail glass; Water Capacity: 90 grams
E – White, red and green glass; Water Capacity: 100 grams
F – Red glass; Water Capacity: 60 grams
G – Flute glass; Water Capacity: 30 grams

Each recipe states a letter referring to the glass to be used.

# VERRES A EMPLOYER ET LEUR CONTENANCE

**A**
**Verre à mélange**
Contenance Eau : 500 grammes.

**B**
**Verre à Cobbler, rouge et blanc**
Contenance Eau : 250 gr.

**C**
**Gobelet blanc, rouge et vert**
Contenance Eau : 125 gr.

**D**
**Verre à Cocktail**
Contenance Eau : 90 grammes.

**E**
**Verre blanc, rouge et vert**
Contenance Eau : 100 grammes.

**F**
**Verre rouge**
Contenance Eau : 60 gr.

**G**
**Verre flûte** Contenance Eau : 30 gr.

**Chaque Recette indique par une lettre le Verre qu'il faut employer**

(Louis Fouquet endorsement courtesy of Greg Boehm.)

FIRST PART

# COCKTAILS

AND

## How to prepare them

# USTENSILES POUR COCKTAILS

Figure 2

**Cuillère à Cocktail**
Pièce... **5** fr.

**Bouchon**
Pièce.. **3** fr.

Figure 3

**Bouteille à Bitter** Angostura
Avec bouchon stilligoutte
Pièce...... **7** fr. **50**

Figure 4

**Cuillère passoire**
Pièce... **9** fr.

Figure 5

**Gobelet à Cocktail**
Avec Couvercle à passoire

Pièce................. **26** francs

FIRST PART

# COCKTAILS

The cocktail, a precious beverage so admired by all our fine gourmets, is one of the best aperitifs when done according to the rules of art.

The "Cock-a-tailer" so named a cocktail by the Italians, is essentially an American beverage and its mixing is the first lesson to give to a young barman before moving on to other various drinks that do not require so much care and refinement.

To make a good cocktail it is a must to have a table filled with the following:

1° A few decanters with dasher tops for essences (see figure 3), to pour dashes and which will contain: Cusenier absinthe—Cusenier curaçao—Cusenier crème de noyaux—Angostura—orange bitters and quinquina extract, etc.;

2° A mixing glass (see glass A, page 22) with a rather strong base to resist shocks from the spoon you will mix the liquid with;

3° A spoon with a rounded base (page 26), to ease the mixing;

4° A strainer (page 26) to separate the ice from the drink before serving;

5° A silver cocktail shaker (page 26), with a straining lid for individuals who desire a shaken cocktail.

Last, to make a good cocktail here's how you must proceed:

Take your mixing glass, place some ice cubes in it, take your decanters with dasher tops by the neck, between the middle and index fingers and pour your specified essences per dashes, then the preferred spirit for your cocktail: cognac or whisky or gin, etc.

Then mix with your cocktail spoon, use the strainer and pour into the glass without letting any ice cubes go through. If your eye is good, you should fill the glass exactly, without a drop remaining in your mixing glass.

If you don't trust yourself, make your cocktail in the serving glass, then empty it carefully into the mixing glass to chill the liquid properly and then transfer it back to the first glass. That way you won't have any left over. This method is mainly employed by people who don't practice often. During busy hours the first method will save you time, but it requires a dexterity which you will only obtain by practising a lot.

When your cocktail is served, delicately cut a fine sliver of lemon zest and half break it lengthwise over the liquid to extract the oil. Then let it sink to the bottom of the glass. In that manner your cocktail has a light lemon perfume which is always appreciated. I have often seen bartenders squeezing the lemon zest outside of the glass and then placing it in the cocktail, believing that it is for the eyes only and that the cocktail does not need this last refinement. It is a big mistake.

When you serve a cocktail to a lady, it is always better to rim the glass with sugar by slightly rubbing the sides on a freshly cut lemon slice and then dipping it delicately in powdered sugar, which gives a frosty effect and kindly flatters the lips and the eyes.

For shaken cocktails, you need to use a cocktail goblet (page 26) instead of the mixing glass and shake hard up and down with two hands. Then you have a cocktail heavily iced, but not as pleasant as the previous method.

Well, the cocktail has definitely been adopted and nursed into the American culture and for quite some time. But is the drink really an American invention?

Various linguistic sources mention a "coquetel" as a rich and stimulating beverage for some centuries in France, composed of wine—Bordeaux, Bourgogne, Champagne—depending on the region, a small amount of good quality locally produced eau-de-vie, egg yolk and sugar served in a cup.

In the late 1770s, General Lafayette took off from Bordeaux to America with the libation, where it was bastardized to "cocktail" in English. He visited Albany, New York, a short distance from Vermont where the earliest use of the word appeared, and passed through or very near Hudson, New York, where *The Balance and Columbian Repository* was published.

Notice as you proceed into the recipes, the classic cocktail ingredients (gin, vermouth, champagne, whisky, etc....) listed below are all mixed with Louis' touch of noyaux and curaçao in similar manners with a different amount of dashes to suit the spirit, which makes them all very balanced and well-structured aperitifs.

## N° 1   ALABAZAM COCKTAIL
### GLASS D

Place some ice cubes in mixing glass A, add 4 dashes of Angostura, 8 dashes of curaçao, 4 drops of lemon juice. Fill up with Curlier cognac [50 ml], mix well with a spoon, strain into the glass, garnish with a lemon zest and serve.

> The Alabazam Cocktail is also listed in the *American & other Drinks* by Leo Engel, published in 1878, as one of his specialties made at The Criterion in London.
>
> They are similar recipes, but Leo's adds white sugar, which makes a less harsh version than Louis'.

## N° 2   ABSINTHE COCKTAIL
### GLASS C

Place some ice cubes in mixing glass A, add 4 dashes of Angostura, 2 dashes of curaçao, 1 coffee spoon [1 barspoon] of anisette, Cusenier white absinthe and water in equal quantity [50 ml each], mix well, strain into the glass, garnish with a lemon zest and serve.

N.B.—It is preferable to use white absinthe to the green because of the colour given to the mixture, the taste is absolutely the same, but the white one gives a beautiful pink colour and the green a greyish colour and very unappetizing.

> Most of Louis' peers did not mention the quality of absinthe they were mixing, and his drink does indeed have an unusual cloudy pink hue. Also most bartenders of the time were using gomme syrup as opposed to orange curaçao which gives a drier fragrance to this classic cocktail.
>
> I would suggest preparing the mixture without ice to avoid crystallizing the absinthe, and then stir gently over ice.

## N°3   ANGLER'S COCKTAIL
### GLASS D

Place some ice cubes in the mixing glass A, add 3 dashes of Angostura, 6 dashes of orange [bitters], 1 coffee spoon [1 barspoon] of raspberry syrup, finish with gin [60 ml], mix, strain into the glass, garnish with a lemon zest and serve.

The Angler's Cocktail is a bitter drink, I found the same recipe in Charlie Paul's *Recipes of American and other Iced Drinks* which was published in 1902.

Decreasing the bitters to 1 dash of Angostura and 2 of Orange will work in favour along the raspberry syrup and the gin.

In 1922, Robert Vermeire of the Embassy Club in London included in his third version of *Cocktails How to Mix Them* the Angler Cocktail:

'This cocktail is very popular in Bohemia and Czecho-Slovakia. It was introduced by V.P. Himmelreich. The ingredients are put in the mixing glass with broken ice:

2 dashes of Angostura Bitters

2 dashes of Orange Bitters

1/6 gill of Vantogrio [a local non-alcoholic syrup].

2/6 gill of Gin

Stir up with a spoon. Strain into a cocktail-glass. Squeeze lemon-peel on top.

Another version appearing in the 1937 *UKBG Approved Cocktails* manual, included Hercules, an herbal aniseed liqueur made in Britain instead of the raspberry syrup. This version tends to be more popular nowadays but rather different from Louis'.

## N°4   APPETIZER COCKTAIL
### GLASS D

Place some ice cubes in mixing glass A, add 4 dashes of Angostura, 1 coffee spoon [1 barspoon] of powdered sugar, 2 dashes of lemon juice finish with Scotch whisky [60 ml], mix, strain into the glass, garnish with a lemon zest and serve.

A different Appetizer Cocktail appeared in 1895, in *Modern American Drinks* by George K. Kappeler, made of 3 dashes of absinthe, 3 dashes of pepsin bitters [a gastric stimulant digestive at 25% ABV made in Chicago], 1 jigger of vermouth. Louis' version is more similar to a classic Scotch cocktail with a hint lemon for freshness.

### N°5    BRANDY COCKTAIL
#### GLASS D
Place some ice cubes in mixing glass A, and add 2 dashes of Angostura, 3 dashes of crème de noyaux, 3 dashes of Cusenier curaçao, finish with [50 ml] Curlier fine champagne cognac, mix and strain into the glass, garnish with a lemon zest and serve.

### N°6    BOURBON WHISKY COCKTAIL
#### GLASS D
Place some ice cubes in mixing glass A, add 2 dashes of Angostura, 4 dashes of crème de noyaux, 3 dashes of curaçao, finish with [50 ml] Bourbon Whisky, mix and strain into the glass, garnish with a lemon zest and serve.

### N°7    BOMBAY COCKTAIL
#### GLASS D
Place some ice cubes in mixing glass A, add 3 dashes of Angostura, 3 dashes of crème de noyaux, 4 dashes of curaçao, 1 coffee spoon [1 barspoon] of powdered sugar, finish with Curlier cognac [60 ml], mix well, strain into the glass, garnish with a lemon zest and serve.

Louis' own take on a Brandy Cocktail with the addition of sugar and an extra dash of Angostura which gives more body to the drink. I also recommend using more cognac [60 ml] to preserve balance of the drink.

With less spirit, the drink becomes flat and candy-like with little character.

## N° 8   CHAMPAGNE COCKTAIL
### GLASS C

Place an ice cube in the C glass and add 3 dashes of curaçao, 2 dashes of Angostura bitters and a lemon zest. Fill up [100 ml] with Henriot Sillery dry champagne, mix slightly add some straws and serve.

This makes a very dry Champagne Cocktail. I would suggest adding the usual bitter soaked sugar to sweeten it and slowly release the Angostura.

Curaçao works really well here.

## N° 9   COFFEE COCKTAIL
### GLASS C

Place some ice cubes in mixing glass A, add 3 dashes of gomme syrup, 4 dashes of crème de noyaux, 1 mouth spoon [10 ml] Curlier fine champagne cognac, finish with coffee [60 ml], mix well, strain into the glass, sprinkle some nutmeg and serve in the C glass.

The recipe above has not much body and lacks cognac flavours. To improve it a little, increase the gomme to 5 ml, the cognac to 30 ml and decrease the coffee to 45 ml. Of course it depends on what type of coffee that you use. The coffee and nutmeg aroma combination work so well in that drink.

## N° 10  CHINESE COCKTAIL
### GLASS D

Place some ice cubes in mixing glass A, add 2 dashes of Angostura, 4 dashes of crème de noyaux, 4 dashes of curaçao, 1 coffee spoon [1 barspoon] of powdered sugar, finish with Curlier cognac and rum in equal quantity [30 ml each], mix well, strain into the glass, garnish with a lemon zest and serve.

Similar to the Bombay Cocktail but with a more fiery spirit, rum instead of cognac, which makes this a more pungent alternative.

In 1902, Charlie Paul listed the Chinese Cocktail but omitted the rum, noyaux, and curaçao which to me is the same recipe as a Brandy Cocktail.

In 1904, Franck Newman came up with another recipe for the Chinese Cocktail:

3 dashes of Angostura
3 dashes of curaçao
3 dashes of maraschino
6 drops of grenadine
1 liqueur glass of rum
Shake with crushed ice and strain into a glass.

This recipe was soon popularised by Robert Vermeire and Harry McElhone.

## N° 11  EAST INDIA COCKTAIL
### GLASS D

Place some ice cubes in mixing glass A, add 1 coffee spoon [1 barspoon] of curaçao, pineapple syrup and maraschino, 3 dashes of Angostura, finish with Curlier cognac [60 ml], mix, strain into the glass, garnish with a lemon zest and serve.

The first version of the East India Cocktail appeared in 1882, in Harry Johnson's *Bartender's Manual* as it is listed above. Harry recommends using red curaçao for colour in his recipe. Using orange curaçao won't make much difference in taste. He also mentions this drink is a great favourite with the English living in East India.

In *The Modern Bartenders' Guide* by O. H. Byron, published in 1884, the pineapple syrup is replaced by raspberry syrup which gives a less exotic sensation but also very good.

If you can't find any pineapple syrup you can always use cartoned or tinned pineapple juice by upgrading the measure to 2 barspoons or 10 ml.

## N° 12    GIN COCKTAIL
### GLASS D

Place some ice cubes in mixing glass A, add 3 dashes of Angostura bitters, 3 dashes of crème de noyaux, 3 dashes of curaçao, finish with old gin [50 ml], mix, strain into the glass, garnish with a lemon zest and serve.

I tried it with aged and unaged oude genever. Both work in this drink, the unaged giving—as expected—a cleaner drink and the aged offering a fuller, dirtier almost olive-brine taste.

## N° 13    IRISH WHISKY COCKTAIL
### GLASS D

Place some ice cubes in mixing glass A, add 2 dashes of Angostura, 3 dashes of crème de noyaux, 3 dashes of curaçao, finish with gin [50 ml], mix, strain into the glass, garnish with a lemon zest and serve.

The above is an obvious typographical error. However, it had to be tested as written and as it should have been.

Made according to the recipe this drink is well balanced, using the freshness of a gin as opposed to genever works well with this recipe following a typical Fouquet formula.

Made with actual Irish whiskey however, and following the same
measurements the drink remains balanced, with different depth of
character and a more mellow finish.

## N° 14   JAPANESE COCKTAIL
### GLASS D

Place some ice cubes in mixing glass A, add 2 dashes of Angostura
bitters, 3 dashes of crème de noyaux, 3 dashes of curaçao, 1 small spoon
[flat barspoon] of orgeat syrup, finish with Curlier cognac [60 ml],
mix, strain into the glass, garnish with a lemon zest and serve.

Invented by Professor Jerry Thomas to celebrate the arrival of New
York's first Japanese embassy, this drink takes a creamy and rounded
element from the orgeat which results in a softer drink.

## N° 15   JERSEY COCKTAIL
### GLASS C

Place some ice cubes in mixing glass A, add 1 small spoon
[flat barspoon] of powdered sugar, 3 dashes of Angostura, 1 dash of
curaçao, 1 dash of crème de noyaux, 1 small spoon [flat barspoon] of
Curlier cognac, finish with cider [100 ml], mix, strain into the glass,
garnish with a lemon zest and serve.

A dry cider is an absolute. The apple flavours work really well with
the other ingredients. Even the small amount of cognac adds some aged
character. It is also featured in Jerry Thomas' 1862 bar manual.

## N° 16   LADIE'S COCKTAIL
### RED GLASS D

Place some ice cubes in mixing glass A, add 1 small barspoon
[flat barspoon] of powdered sugar and anisette, 3 dashes of green
crème de menthe, 3 dashes of curaçao, finish with kirsch and water

in equal quantity [30 ml each], mix, strain into the glass, garnish with an orange slice and serve.

> This cocktail is very different from the ones before. Using new ingredients such as kirsch and crème de menthe, Fouquet created a drink that appears very avant-garde for the time. Whilst we would most likely now attribute the crystalline bright blue colour and orange slice garnish to the 1980s, when placed in context this is a very interesting and creative drink worth trying out. The name alludes to this as something colourful and refreshing for the ladies.

## N° 17   LOUIS' QUINA COCKTAIL
### GLASS D

Place some ice cubes in mixing glass A, add 6 dashes of quinine extract, 2 dashes of curaçao, finish with Quinquina Dubonnet [60 ml], mix, strain into the glass, garnish with a lemon zest and serve.

> At the time, Quinquina Dubonnet contained a higher level of quinine, so this would have been a very bitter drink. Nowadays, the level of quinine in Dubonnet is lower and consequently the cocktail is rounder than it would have been originally.
>
> Quinquina tincture is not available any more, but you can always make your own by infusing some quinine bark to some vodka or white rum. The most readily available substitute is a dash of Angostura bitters.

## N° 18   MARTINI COCKTAIL
### GLASS D

The most pleasing of the cocktails when we observe well the following quantities:

Place some ice cubes in mixing glass A, add 4 dashes of orange bitter, 2 dashes of absinthe, 3 dashes of curaçao, 3 dashes of crème de noyaux, finish with gin and Turin vermouth in equal quantity [30 ml each] mix, strain into the glass, garnish with a lemon zest and serve.

Another well-balanced and innovative cocktail from Louis here.
It makes good sense to use absinthe and orange bitters instead of
Angostura to complement the gin.

### N° 19   MANHATTAN COCKTAIL
#### GLASS D

Place some ice cubes in mixing glass A, add 2 dashes of Angostura,
2 dashes of noyaux, 3 dashes of curaçao, finish with rye whiskey and
Turin vermouth in equal quantity [30 ml each], mix, strain into the
glass, garnish with a lemon zest and serve.

The noyaux here adds an extra level to the flavours. It remains
however, a very light palatable drink.

### N° 20   MARTINICAN VERMOUTH COCKTAIL
#### GLASS D

Place some ice cubes in mixing glass A, add 2 dashes of
Angostura, 2 dashes of curaçao, 2 dashes of noyaux, 1 small spoon
[flat barspoon] of pineapple syrup, finish with Turin vermouth and
rum in equal quantity [30 ml each], mix, strain into the glass, garnish
with a lemon zest and serve.

This is basically Louis' evolution of a Martini, or Manhattan with
a hint of pineapple syrup which works very well with rum. A similar
Martinican Cocktail is listed in *American-Bar* by Franck Newman in 1904,
without pineapple nor noyaux.

### N° 21   MORNING GLORY COCKTAIL
#### GLASS C

Place some ice cubes in mixing glass A, add 2 dashes of Angostura,
3 dashes of noyaux, 3 dashes of curaçao, 1 dash of Cusenier absinthe,
1 small spoon [flat barspoon] of powdered sugar, then pour some

Scotch whisky and Curlier cognac in equal quantity [30 ml each], mix, strain into the glass, garnish with a lemon zest, finish seltzer water and serve.

This is a very interesting drink, though not one of the most enjoyable in this book. Each ingredient is important to the overall elements within the drink. For instance, the cognac acts to round out the Scotch flavours in what could potentially be a rather harsh, strong cocktail.

### N°22   NAPOLÉON'S OWN COCKTAIL
#### GLASS C

Place some ice cubes in mixing glass A, add 1 small spoon [flat barspoon] of powdered sugar, one of lemon juice, whisky and gin in equal quantity [30 ml], mix, strain into the glass, garnish with a lemon zest. Fill up with siphon and serve.

This seemed like a dangerous mixture, but is actually a Scotch and soda with a fresher element to it.

### N°23   RYE WHISKY COCKTAIL
#### GLASS D

Place some ice cubes in mixing glass A, add 3 dashes of curaçao, 3 dashes of noyaux, 2 dashes of Angostura, finish with rye whisky [60 ml], mix, strain into the glass, garnish with a lemon zest and serve.

### N°24   SHERRY COCKTAIL
#### GLASS D
#### (Xérès wine cocktail)

Place some ice cubes in mixing glass A, add 3 dashes of curaçao, 3 dashes of noyaux, 2 dashes of Angostura, finish with Sandeman sherry [50 ml], mix, strain and pour, garnish with a lemon zest and serve.

> Funnily enough, the sherry impacts the flavours within the cocktail and takes the majority of the weight in this drink. The other notes come across as a fragrant addition to the sherry base.

## N°25   LOUIS' SPECIAL COCKTAIL
### GLASS D

Place some ice cubes in mixing glass A, add 3 dashes of curaçao, noyaux and Angostura, pour half gin [30 ml] and half Turin vermouth [30 ml], squeeze half an orange [30 ml], mix well, strain and pour, garnish with a lemon zest and serve.

> Depth, complexity, freshness. This is Louis' own take on previous cocktails numbered 18, 19 and 20. This drink is a combination of the three. Observing his well used trilogy and the addition of orange juice, soon to become an unquestionable classic: the Bronx Cocktail.

## N°26   SODA COCKTAIL
### GLASS B

The Soda Cocktail is especially recommended for delicate stomachs. Before a meal, it will give appetite if one already has a heavy stomach from various aperitifs. After, it will aid digestion and, drunk at once, it will serve a gentle freshness throughout the body and restore the digestive and nutritive functions to order.

In the cobbler glass B place an ice chunk, add 6 dashes of Angostura, 4 dashes of curaçao, 2 dashes of noyaux, squeeze a lemon zest and pour a soda that has not lost its gas. When drinking, mix it with a coffee spoon [1 barspoon] of powdered sugar and drink in one go at the effervescence moment.

This is a refreshing, delightful long mixed drink. Make sure you follow Louis' instructions for consumption for the full effect!

## N°27  SARATOGA COCKTAIL
### GLASS D

Place some ice cubes in mixing glass A, add 2 dashes of Angostura, curaçao and noyaux, finish with cognac Curlier, Scotch whisky and vermouth in equal quantities [20 ml each] mix well, strain into the glass, garnish with a lemon slice and serve.

The Saratoga Cocktail is a bit of a wild beast as most bartenders have different take on it. Louis' version follows Jerry Thomas' school with the addition of his favourite essences which make it perfectly balanced, silky smooth with a hint of smoke. It is a really good homogenisation of flavours.

## N°28  VERMOUTH COCKTAIL
### GLASS D

Place some ice cubes in mixing glass A, add 2 dashes of Angostura, 3 of noyaux and 4 of curaçao, finish with Turin vermouth [60 ml] mix well, strain into the glass, garnish lemon zest and serve.

## N°29  VICTORIA COCKTAIL
### GLASS D

Place some ice cubes in mixing glass A, add 1 small spoon [1 barspoon] of powdered sugar, 6 dashes of green crème de menthe, finish with cognac Curlier and rum in equal quantities [30 ml each] mix well, strain into the glass, garnish with a stalk of peppermint or an orange slice, depending of the season and serve.

This recipe creates a sickly-sweet candy style drink. Perhaps a better choice for after dinner than before, an orange slice is preferable as a garnish to introduce a finer aroma and a hint of citrus. Rhum agricole works much better, as it highlights the flavours of the cognac and the mint.

## N° 30   WHISKY COCKTAIL
### GLASS D

Place some ice cubes in mixing glass A, add 3 dashes of Angostura, noyaux, curaçao, finish with Scotch whisky [60 ml], mix well, strain into the glass, garnish with a lemon zest and serve.

SECOND PART

# SHORT DRINKS

AND

How to prepare them

# SHORT DRINKS

Short drinks. So are named all these imaginative beverages served at any time of day, which we can imbibe without fear before and after the meals. Generally served in medium size (glasses E, C, F, and G), their composition is remarkable. A great number of them are made with the yolk or the white of an egg. These are excellent for the stomach and often ordered by skilled doctors whose customers are too gourmet to go without a drink between meals, because of stomach ache or other troubles, often due to the abuse of bad alcohol or harmful bitters rather than hygienic concoctions.

To make all these precious compositions, it is necessary to add to your sideboard some other tools essential for the success of all these mixes.

It is good to have:

1°   A series of silver goblets, fitting each other to be able to shake strongly as shown in figure n° 1 (page 49)

2°   A spice container (page 49), in which we'll put the nutmeg powder, in order to sprinkle the beverages that requires;

3° An egg white beater like the ones in all households;

4° A series of glasses E, C, F, and G, of different colours that must be used when the greyish colour of a mix requires.

Like cocktails, people who can't free pour directly into the silver cups will do better by directly preparing them into the serving glass shown. Then shake them to re-pour afterwards, while always being careful to strain the ice.

Mr Fouquet's introduction to the short drink section recommends four type of glassware to serve those libations. In truth, you will need another two: the cobbler and cocktail glass are also used.

In this chapter you will find a series of sours, flips, fizzes, eye-openers for the morning after, and pousse cafés which were a fine tradition in France.

He includes some very simple sweetened spirit recipes like brandy and honey or gin and molasses which could refer to the original style of slings. Some more complex multi-layered, egg yolk suspensions and foam finishes also appear in this part.

Pour frapper une Boisson

## UTENSILS FOR THE COMPOSITION OF SHORT DRINKS

Spices container
Piece............... 6fr.

Nutmeg Grater
Piece ........... 15fr.

Drinks Goblets (3 sizes)
The set .......... 70fr.

# USTENSILES POUR LA COMPOSITION
# DES SHORT DRINKS

**Flacon** pour Epices

Pièce.............. 6 fr.

**Râpe à Muscade**

Pièce.. ........... 15 fr.

Figure 1

**Gobelets pour Boissons** (3 grandeurs)

Le jeu......... **70** fr.

## N°31   BOSOM CARESSER
### GLASS B

Place some ice cubes in a silver goblet, add a fresh egg yolk, 1 coffee spoon of grenadine and maraschino [5 ml each], 1 mouth spoon [10 ml] of Curlier cognac, finish with [50 ml] sherry and shake well by adjusting a bigger size goblet on the top, strain into the glass and serve.

A fruity and aromatic concoction, the cognac is there to give a little kick to this sherry-berry caresser.

## N°32   BLACK STRIPE
### PINK GLASS B

Place some ice chunks in a silver goblet, add 2 coffee spoons [10 ml] of molasses, finish with water [20 ml] and Scotch whisky [60 ml], shake well, strain into the glass then sprinkle with nutmeg and serve.

A common drink of the epoch usually made with rum, served over fine ice for the summer and hot during the winter.

Louis' version doesn't really work for me. The molasses is too potent to bind nicely with the Scotch.

If you want to use Scotch though, try recipe N° 52. The suggested methods and recipe seemed to offer a better result.

## N°33   BRANDY SHANTERALLA
### YELLOW GLASS E

Place some ice chunks in a silver goblet, add 1 mouth spoon [10 ml] of curaçao, 1 mouth spoon [10 ml] of yellow chartreuse, 2 mouth spoons [20 ml] of anisette, 1 coffee spoon [1 barspoon] powdered sugar, finish with [40 ml] Curlier cognac, shake well, strain into the glass and serve.

A lot going on in this drink but all the flavours integrate beautifully. It is still a tiny bit sweet but well balanced. Omitting the powdered sugar would result in a drier style. As is, it is a great after dinner drink.

## N°34   BOMBAY PUNCHET
### YELLOW GLASS E

Place some ice in a silver goblet, add 1 coffee spoon [1 barspoon] powdered sugar, 4 dashes of maraschino, 4 dashes of lemon juice, liqueur glass [15 ml] Curlier cognac and finish with [45 ml] Sandeman sherry, shake well, strain into the glass and serve.

A light and zingy concoction, this drink is a delightful aperitif.

## N°35   BRANDY DAISY
### CLEAR GLASS C

Place some ice in a silver goblet, add 1 coffee spoon [1 barspoon] powdered sugar, 3 dashes of lemon juice, 1 squirt of soda siphon, 1 liqueur glass [30 ml] of yellow Chartreuse and finish with some [30 ml] cognac Curlier, shake well, strain into the glass and serve.

Harry Johnson's invention, the daisy, is made with yellow Chartreuse. This a really delightful concoction. It has superb balance. The hint of lemon combines with the herbal toned chartreuse and the soft oaky cognac. Bravo!

## N°36   BOSTON FLIP
### CLEAR GLASS C

Place some ice in a silver goblet, add 1 spoon [1 barspoon] of powdered sugar, break a whole fresh egg, finish with [50 ml] rye whiskey, shake hard, strain into the glass then sprinkle a little nutmeg on the top and serve.

A classic flip, the whole egg helps cover some of the aggressive notes of the rye whiskey.

## N° 37   BRANDY AND HONEY
### CLEAR GLASS C

Place some ice cubes in the glass and add 1 coffee spoon [5 ml] of honey, fill it with Curlier cognac [50 ml], mix well with a spoon, garnish with a lemon slice and serve.

It is so simple that the name gives it away. Perfect after dinner for pleasant nightcap. I would suggest making honey water (equal parts honey and water) beforehand to aid the mixing, and add 2 barspoons (10 ml) to the recipe. It also adds a bit of dilution to the drink, providing a better balance.

## N° 38   BRANDY SCAFFA
### GLASS G

Pour slowly in the glass half maraschino liqueur and half cognac [15 ml each], add 2 dashes of  Angostura bitters on the top and serve.

A scaffa is an old time mixed drink where the ingredients are simply added into the glass without stirring or shaking. It was very popular from the 1860s until the early 1920s as ice was not as plentiful in bars. It is a distinctly masculine drink as they are undiluted and very strong. It takes its name from an old Norse term meaning 'to make something yourself' which is appropriate since this is a very simple drink to make.

## N° 39   BRANDY CHAMPARELLE
### GLASS G

Slowly pour in equal proportions: curaçao, yellow Chartreuse, anisette, kirsch or Curlier cognac.

It is preferable to pour the ingredients across the back of a spoon to avoid mixing them. They should remain perfectly distinct from one to another like in a pousse café. I believe that this recipe comes from the 1882 Harry Johnson bartender's manual though he spelled the name "Shamparelle". Harry also recommended a red curaçao to layer into the drink.

## N°40   BRANDY FLIP
### CLEAR GLASS C

Place some ice in a silver goblet, add 3 dashes of curaçao, 3 dashes of noyaux, 1 coffee spoon [1 barspoon] of powdered sugar, break an egg, use the yolk, finish with [60 ml] cognac Curlier, shake hard, strain into the glass then sprinkle a little nutmeg on top and serve.

Rich nutty liqueur combined with dry bitter orange and fine cognac is the perfect combination for a velvety flip.

## N°41   SPECIAL COFFEE COCKTAIL
### CLEAR GLASS C

This cocktail is a Short Drink well appreciated by the Americans as a digestif and must be served extremely cold.

Place some ice in a silver goblet, add 2 dashes of curaçao, 2 dashes of noyaux, 1 fresh egg, 1 coffee spoon [1 barspoon] of powdered sugar, finish with Sandeman ruby port and Curlier cognac [30 ml each], shake hard, strain into the glass then sprinkle a little nutmeg on top and serve.

Here is quite an original American beverage because neither coffee nor bitters can be found in its composition. Instead, the name comes from its colour which is exactly like coffee when it is well executed like I indicate above.

This is commonly known as a Coffee Cocktail. Perhaps Louis felt the touches of curaçao and noyaux gave it another dimension and enough depth of flavour to make it special.

As mentioned above and by Professor Jerry Thomas, this is not a true cocktail by American rules but it is a *coquetel* by French rules.

## N°42   CORPSE REVIVER
### GLASS G

This imaginative beverage is very original and very difficult to make since all the products, sold in different outlets, are never of the desired alcohol density. Here is the composition of this beverage: It is preferable to pour each of them on the back of a spoon, not to mix anything, 13 successive liqueurs and by their colour which should be perfectly distinct from one another: grenadine, framboise, anisette, raspberry liqueur, white crème de menthe, green chartreuse, cherry brandy, prunelle, kummel, guignolet [a wild cherry liqueur], kirsch and cognac Curlier.

It is easy to layer these liqueurs by trying several times or weighing them before employing them, in order to get a good result.

Corpse Revivers were a category of drinks more than a single recipe, they originated in the 1870s and were very popular in England and France as a morning "pick–me–up", also called "eye-opener", "reviver", or a "hair of the dog" for those who were suffering from a hangover wanted to ease the pain with a little more of what bit them the night before.

A Corpse Reviver is a bartender's signature drink. They can vary from short and aromatic to sour style and to pousse café style like Louis is suggesting above. They are usually very high in alcohol.

## N°43   COAXER
### CLEAR GLASS C

Place some ice cubes in a silver goblet, add 1 coffee spoon [1 barspoon] of powdered sugar, squeeze half a lemon [15 ml], a fresh egg white and finish with Scotch whisky [60 ml], shake well, strain into the glass and serve.

> In other words, this is a whisky sour with egg white, made in very similar fashion as it is nowadays in London, omitting the bitters. I believe this was one of Louis's inventions. Silky gentle and nicely sour, I highly recommend it.

## N°44   CHAMPAGNE SOUR
### CLEAR GLASS C

Place some ice cubes in a silver goblet, add 1 coffee spoon [1 barspoon] of powdered sugar, 2 dashes of lemon juice, a little water [10 ml], shake well, strain into the glass. Fill up the glass with champagne, garnish with an orange slice, pineapple chunk, some seasonal fruits, straws and serve.

> That number appeared during the early 1880s and is made in similar manner to other sours of that time. The sourness is not very pronounced but brings a nice refreshing lightness to the drink.

## N°45   COLUMBIA SKIN
### RED GLASS E

Place some ice in a silver goblet, add 1 coffee spoon [1 barspoon] of powdered sugar, 2 dashes of lemon juice, a little water [10 ml], finish with [50 ml] rum, shake well, strain into the glass, garnish with a lemon slice and serve.

> This is an interesting recipe to appear a couple of years before the daiquiri, isn't it? Although the ingredients sound like a daiquiri, the combination suggested by Louis' recipe is actually a different drink. The rum adds a silky predominant flavour and texture and the light sweet & sour act in the background as a freshener. Essentially, it is a skin as the name implies.

## N°46   EGG SOUR
### CLEAR GLASS C

Place some small ice cubes in a silver goblet, add 4 dashes of Angostura, a small spoon [flat barspoon] of powdered sugar, 1 whole fresh egg, 1 small liqueur glass of Curlier cognac [20 ml], 1 coffee spoon [5 ml] of gomme syrup, finish with [15 ml] lemon juice, shake well, strain into the glass and serve.

> Even though a small liqueur glass is recommended as a cognac measure, a full liqueur glass [60 ml] works better. It is a great egg sour, everything works beautifully. The whole egg and two types of sugar build an amazing texture together.

## N°47   EGG FLIP
### CLEAR GLASS C

Place some small ice cubes in a silver goblet, add 1 fresh egg yolk, 2 dashes of curaçao, 2 dashes of noyaux, 2 coffee spoons [2 barspoons] of powdered sugar, finish with equal amounts of Curlier cognac and Sandeman sherry [30 ml each], shake well, strain into the glass then sprinkle a little nutmeg on top and serve.

> This is a drier and fresher version of the special Coffee Cocktail with apple and pear flavours from the sherry. Delicious.

## N°48   EYE OPENER
### CLEAR GLASS C

Place some small ice cubes in a silver goblet, add 1 spoon of powdered sugar [1 barspoon], 1 whole fresh egg, finish with cognac and rum [30 ml each], shake well, strain into the glass then sprinkle a little nutmeg on top and serve.

Rum, cognac and fresh egg in the morning will open more than an eye. Like the Corpse Reviver, every bartender had their own secret recipe to wake up the patrons and mend their hangovers back in those days.

## N°49   FOUQUET'S POUSSE-CAFÉ
### GLASS G

In the glass, pour slowly on the back of a spoon: kirsch, curaçao and Curlier fine champagne cognac.

You might want to build the drink in this order: curaçao, cognac and kirsch. The layers will work better. Pousse cafés were very popular in France, usually served beside the coffee after a meal to aid digestion.

## N°50   GIN SOUR
### CLEAR GLASS C

Place some small ice cubes in a silver goblet, add 1 spoon [1 barspoon] of powdered sugar, 2 mouth spoons lemon juice [20 ml], finish with half gin and half water [30 ml each], shake well, strain into the glass, garnish with a half slice of lemon and serve.

My first impression was that this drink was going to be too sharp. Cutting the gin with water is pure genius, resulting in a light and dry concoction with great gin flavours.

## N°51   GOLDEN FIZZ
### CLEAR GLASS C

Place some small ice cubes in a silver goblet, add 1 fresh egg yolk, 2 coffee spoons [2 barspoons] of powdered sugar, finish with some old gin [30 ml] and seltzer water, shake well, strain and pour, garnish with a half lemon slice and serve.

It seems like Louis forgot to include lemon juice in his Golden Fizz. You might want to add 2 mouth spoons [20 ml] to recreate a traditional fizz. Louis' version is quite a mouthful, the lemon is definitely necessary to bring lightness and balance to the drink.

## N° 52   GIN AND MOLASSES
### CLEAR GLASS C

In the glass, add 1 coffee spoon [5 ml] of gomme syrup, 1 spoon [5 ml] of molasses, pour the gin [60 ml] without filling up the glass, in order to allow the customer to pour the water as he desires, and serve.

This blend did not appeal to me at first. Then I made a molasses water (equal parts water and molasses) and followed Louis' instructions, but instead of adding water I shook it with ice. To my surprise it turned out to be delightful.

## N° 53   GIN FIZZ
### CLEAR GLASS C

Place some small ice cubes in a silver goblet, add 1 mouth spoon [10 ml] of lemon juice, 1 liqueur glass [30 ml] of gin, shake well, strain and pour. Fill up with seltzer water, garnish with a half lemon slice and serve.

Well, this time Louis omits the sugar which makes this more of a Lemon Rickey than a Gin Fizz. You might want to add a little sugar or simple syrup into the mix to achieve the balance.

## N° 54   GIN FLIP
### CLEAR GLASS C

Place some small ice cubes in a silver goblet, add 2 coffee spoons [2 barspoons] of powdered sugar, 1 fresh egg yolk, 2 dashes of noyaux, finish with [60 ml] old tom gin, shake well, strain into the glass then sprinkle a little nutmeg on top and serve.

The cardamom of the old tom combines wonderfully with the fragrance of the noyaux.

## N° 55   GOLDEN SLIPPER
### RED GLASS F

Fill the glass one-quarter full of yellow chartreuse, carefully add a fresh whole egg yolk, then slowly pour in some Dantzig eau-de-vie and serve.

This is one of the favourite beverages of the American ladies.

I recommend using a quail egg yolk. It will fit perfectly into the glass and it will be much more delicate to imbibe.

The Golden Slipper is believed to be invented by Harry Johnson in New Orleans. Dantzig eau-de-vie is better know as Danziger Goldwasser, which is a root and herb liqueur that originated in Poland. The liqueur contains a suspension of 22-23 karat gold flakes.

## N° 56   "LUCY" POUSSE-CAFÉ
### GLASS G

Fill half of the glass with yellow Chartreuse, half with Curlier cognac. Pour the cognac gently [over the back of a barspoon] so that you do not mix them.

## N° 57   KNICKERBEIN
### GLASS D

Pour a quarter glass of crème de vanille, add a whole egg yolk, and cover slightly with a layer of Benedictine. Fill up the glass with some kummel, 2 dashes of Angostura and serve.

It is essential to pour all the liqueurs very slowly, in order to avoid mixing them.

The Knickerbein became very popular in Germany around the 1920s. The yolk of a small or medium egg is the right size for the glass and the quantity of liqueur.

## N°58   LOUIS' KNICKERBEIN
### GLASS D

Pour a quarter glass of maraschino liqueur, place delicately one egg yolk, then fill the glass carefully with curaçao, kirsch and Curlier cognac, by leaving a gap from the rim of the glass. Beat the egg white until the foam forms stiff peaks. Place it in a pyramid shape on the top of the drink. Then add 2 dashes of curaçao for garnish and serve.

It is preferable to mix the egg foam with sugar or vanilla, in order to perfume and flatter the palate.

Foams are not a new wave of 21st century molecular mixology. Bartenders were making them back in the 1890s in Paris and London.

Bartenders also had their own takes on this drink. Leo Engel from the American Bar at The Criterion in Piccadilly, London—circa 1875—would make his version with curaçao, noyaux, maraschino and port, the yolk of an egg, finished with the froth of the white. He also had particular directions for imbibing this drink:

"1. Pass the glass under the *nostrils* and *inhale the flavour*. —Pause.

"2. Hold the glass *perpendicularly*, close under your mouth, open it *wide*, and suck the froth by drawing a *deep breath*.—Pause again.

"3. *Point* the lips and take *one-third* of the *liquid contents* remaining in the glass without touching the yolk.—Pause once more

"4. Straighten the body, throw the *head backward*, swallow the contents remaining in the glass *all at once*, at the same time *breaking the yolk* in your mouth."

## N°59   KNICKERBOCKER
### CLEAR GLASS C

Place some small ice cubes in a silver goblet, add 1 small spoon [flat barspoon] of lemon juice, 2 spoons of raspberry syrup [10 ml], 4 dashes of curaçao, finish with some old rum [40 ml] and water [20 ml], shake well, strain into the glass and serve.

Most books published in the era recommend Santa Cruz rum—a Spanish colony style—which is light and sharp. This makes sense with the combination of ingredients. The lemon adds lightness to the drink.

## N°60   LADIES BLUSH
### CLEAR GLASS C

Place some ice cubes in a silver goblet, add 1 small liqueur glass [20 ml] of anisette Curlier, 2 dashes of curaçao, finish with some white absinthe [40 ml] and water [20 ml], shake hard, strain into the glass and serve.

This drink does not appear in any other mixed drink books from the era, apart from one: *American & Other Drinks* by Leo Engel (1878). It is a completely different recipe, but Leo also noted it was a "Favourite Drink among the Fair Sex". Anise is a very popular ingredient in drinks around France. We do not know if Louis' version was used for the same purpose, but if you are a fan of anise definitely go for it.

*Anis. Toujours anis.* But the combination of orange curaçao with the white absinthe does release interesting cacao flavours.

## N°61   LAST DRINK
### RED GLASS F

Place some small ice cubes in a mixing glass, pour in equal quantities of Curlier cognac, yellow chartreuse, cherry brandy, ginger brandy, kummel OO, [10 ml each], mix well, strain into the glass coated with sugar on the rim as indicated on page 28 and pour.

This beverage is the American's favourite after a good meal.

This is like putting all your favourite digestive into a glass. As you can imagine, this is a very sweet drink. The flavours are all over the place but kind of work in a way that you get a hint of each of them, the caraway and cherry brandy are the main. I would omit the sugar rim to avoid a diabetic attack.

Also, you easily make this into a bottled cocktail so you can to avoid juggling five bottles at a time. The drink will also gain an integrity of flavours if you do so.

## N° 62   LEAVE IT TO ME
### CLEAR GLASS C

Take a silver goblet, small ice cubes, add 1 small spoon [flat barspoon] of powdered sugar, juice of half a lemon [15 ml], 1 mouth spoon [10 ml] of raspberry syrup, 1 mouth spoon [10 ml] of maraschino, finish with old tom gin [50 ml], shake well, strain into the glass, garnish with a lemon slice and serve.

Raspberry and maraschino is a very well-known combination, and it works beautifully as a sour with old tom gin.

## N° 63   MINUIT 30
### CLEAR GLASS C

Place some small ice cubes in a silver goblet, add 1 coffee spoon [5 ml] of honey, 4 dashes of curaçao, finish with Scotch [50 ml] and Burgundy red wine [25 ml], shake well, strain into the glass and serve.

Use honey water for better mixability: 10 ml will do the job. It is a great drink, soft and rounded with a hint of smoke. The red wine (I recommend Pinot Noir) adds body and a beautiful dark ruby red colour.

## N°64   MAGNOLIA
### CLEAR GLASS C

Place some ice cubes in a silver goblet, add 1 egg yolk, 1 liqueur glass [30 ml] of Curlier fine champagne cognac, 1 coffee spoon [5 ml] of maraschino, 1 coffee spoon [1 barspoon] of powdered sugar, shake well, strain into the glass. Fill the glass up with champagne, slightly mix with a spoon and serve.

Mentioned in the 1878 edition of Leo Engel's book as one of his speciality served at the London's Criterion, his Magnolia (a la Simmons), used orange curaçao instead of maraschino. Considered a nutritious drink, it was recommended for bad appetite.

## N°65   MAIDEN'S BLUSH
### CLEAR GLASS C

Place some ice cubes in a silver goblet, add half a spoon of powdered sugar [1 barspoon], 1 spoon [5 ml] of raspberry syrup, juice of half a lemon [15 ml], 1 liqueur glass of white absinthe [30 ml], 1 half glass [30 ml] of old tom gin, finish with a bit of water [10 ml], shake, strain into the glass, garnish with a lemon slice and serve.

This is a great sour with nicely combined raspberry and anise flavours and a background of juniper and cardamom. Raspberry syrup is a must in this one for the texture.

## N°66   MORNING CALL
### CLEAR GLASS C

Place some small ice cubes in a silver goblet, add 1 small spoon [flat barspoon] of powdered sugar, 6 dashes of curaçao, 4 dashes of Angostura, finish with equal quantities of rum or Curlier cognac and water [40 ml each], shake well, strain into the glass, garnish with a lemon peel cut in a spiral and serve.

This beverage is suitable for the morning, very light with a hint of bitterness and lovely fresh lemon zest nose.

## N°67   NIGHT CAP
### RED GLASS E

Place some ice cubes in a silver goblet, add 1 spoon [1 barspoon] of powdered sugar and pour in equal quantities of soft rum punch, Curlier cognac and water [30 ml each], shake, strain into the glass and serve.

This soft rum punch is a bottled cocktail, very popular from the mid 1800s until the mid 1900s. The rum was sweetened with sugar cane syrup, flavoured with tropical fruits, vanilla and citrus. It was mostly used as a ready-to-drink product and rarely appears as an ingredient in cocktail books.

## N°68   PRAIERIE [sic] OYSTER
### GLASS D

This beverage is recommended for preparing the stomach before a good meal.

Break an egg and place the yolk delicately into the glass, add salt, cayenne pepper, Worcestershire sauce, few drops of good vinegar, finish with sherry and cognac in equal quantity [30 ml each] and serve. It is necessary to take this drink as much as possible in one go.

The Prairie Oyster was introduced by Leo Engel who was a famous bartender at The Criterion in London during the late 1870s which was located at the Spiers and Pond's French opera at The Criterion Theatre.

Probably the cleanest Prairie Oyster out there, it is a great drink. The sherry and cognac work very well. However, I suggest you to stir them over ice before pouring them in.

## N°69   PICK ME UP
### CLEAR GLASS C

Take a silver goblet, ice cubes, add 1 mouth spoon [10 ml] of lemon juice, 1 mouth spoon [10 ml] of grenadine, 1 mouth spoon [10 ml] of old kirsch, shake well, strain into the glass. Fill up the glass with Henriot Sillery dry champagne, add a half orange slice, slightly mix with a spoon and serve.

A well-balanced and refreshing morning drink.

## N°70   POUSSE L'AMOUR
### RED GLASS G

Pour 1 coffee spoon [5 ml] of maraschino, break an egg, delicately add the whole yolk, 4 dashes of curaçao, 4 dashes crème de noyaux, finish with [30 ml] Curlier cognac and serve without mixing.

This beverage must be drunk in one go.

The Pousse L'amour originated in France. There are many recipes around. One of the most popular ones includes maraschino, egg yolk, vanilla cordial and cognac. But others use yellow chartreuse or Benedictine instead of the vanilla.

Here again I would suggest using a quail egg.

## N°71   POUSSE-CAFÉ
### G GLASS

Pour in equal quantities with the back of a barspoon without mixing: anisette, green crème de menthe, cherry brandy, Curlier fine champagne cognac, and serve.

## N°72   POUSSE-CAFÉ PARISIEN
### GLASS G

Prepare it the same way as the recipe above, but with 3 liqueurs: curaçao, kirsch, chartreuse.

## N°73   PORT FLIP
### CLEAR GLASS C

Place some ice cubes in a silver goblet, add 4 dashes of curaçao, 2 dashes of crème de noyaux, 1 small spoon [flat barspoon] of powdered sugar, 1 fresh egg yolk, finished with [60 ml] ruby port, shake hard, strain into the glass, then sprinkle a little nutmeg on top and serve.

## N°74   QUEEN CHARLOTTE
### CLEAR GLASS C

Place some ice cubes in a silver goblet, add 1.5 spoons [1.5 barspoons] of redcurrant syrup, 1 liqueur glass [30 ml] of fine champagne cognac, 3 dashes of crème de noyaux, 2 dashes of curaçao, 1 small spoon [flat barspoon] of crème de menthe, shake well, strain into the glass, finish with seltzer water, garnish with an orange slice and serve.

Not one of the best in the book as the cognac gets a bit disguised. But the redcurrant and crème de menthe combo is really good. I used white crème de menthe for a fresher effect than the green.

## N°75    SQUARE MEAL
### RED GLASS E

Place some ice cubes in a silver goblet, add 1 fresh egg yolk, 3 dashes of curaçao, 2 dashes of crème de noyaux, half a liqueur glass [15 ml] of ginger brandy, finish with [45 ml] fine champagne cognac, shake well, strain into the glass and serve.

> A very fine drink, the ginger brandy works beautifully with the rest of the ingredients. A small barspoon of sugar could help for a sweeter palate.

## N°76    SAM WARD
### GLASS D

Fill up the glass with crushed ice, add some yellow chartreuse [50 ml], cut a long lemon zest and insert it between the glass and the ice, add one maraschino cherry and serve with a straw.

A lot of Americans insist on a small spoon of green crème de menthe before serving.

> This is no less than a chartreuse frappe with a hint of citrus and mint, if required. Sounds like the perfect after dinner drink to me. It was invented at the Manhattan Club in New York.

## N°77    SHERRY FLIP
### CLEAR GLASS C

Place some ice cubes in a silver goblet, add 4 dashes of curaçao, 2 dashes of crème de noyaux, 1 small spoon [flat barspoon] of powdered sugar, 1 fresh egg yolk, finish with sherry [60 ml], shake hard, strain into the glass then sprinkle a little nutmeg on top and serve.

## N°78   SHERRY AND EGG
### YELLOW E GLASS

Break a fresh egg and place the whole yolk delicately into the glass, fill up with dry sherry and serve.

Yuck! Do not try this at home.

## N°79   STARS AND STRIPES
### GLASS G

Pour successively in the glass and without mixing, red crème de noyaux, maraschino, yellow chartreuse, green curaçao and Curlier cognac fine champagne.

Here you are for the stripes. Now for the stars. Drink the glass in one go, pay and leave. You will see the stars. Right at that moment the owner will be happy to close his doors, when his customers are too irritating, because of the lateness of the hour.

Brilliant! I could not have said it better than Louis did.

## N°80   SILVER FIZZ
### CLEAR C GLASS

Place some ice cubes in a silver goblet, add 2 coffee spoons [2 barspoons] of powdered sugar, 1 fresh egg white, 2 liqueur glasses [60 ml] of old gin, shake well, strain into the glass. Fill up with seltzer water, garnish with a half lemon slice and serve.

Like in the Golden Fizz recipe listed earlier, Louis has forgotten to include the lemon juice here to make his Silver Fizz. You might want to add 2 mouth spoons (20 ml) to recreate a traditional fizz.

## N°81   THUNDER
### CLEAR GLASS C

The thunder is served in this manner:

Place some small ice cubes in a silver goblet, add half spoon [half barspoon] of powdered sugar, 1 whole fresh egg, 1 liqueur glass [30 ml] of Curlier cognac, 1 large pinch of cayenne pepper, shake well, strain into the glass and serve.

Silky and smooth to start, soon comes the prickly heat at the back of the mouth on the start of a long burn. Use ground cayenne pepper for a better (or worse) effect.

## N°82   TOO-TOO
### CLEAR GLASS C

Place some ice in a silver goblet, add 1 small spoon [flat barspoon] of powdered sugar, 1 fresh egg, 1 mouth spoon [10 ml] of raspberry syrup, finish with Curlier cognac and rum [30 ml each], shake hard, strain into the glass and serve.

## N°83   WHISKY SOUR
### CLEAR GLASS C

Place some small ice cubes in a silver goblet, add 1 small spoon [flat barspoon] of powdered sugar, 2 mouth spoon [20 ml] lemon juice. Fill up with water and Scotch whisky in equal quantities [30 ml each], shake, strain into the glass, garnish with a half lemon slice and serve.

This one is on the sharp side. A full barspoon of sugar will establish a better balance.

### N°84   WHISKY FLASH
#### CLEAR GLASS C

Place some small ice cubes in a silver goblet, add 1 spoon of powdered sugar [1 barspoon], 1 mouth spoon [10 ml] of lemon juice, 2 mouth spoons [20 ml] of pineapple syrup, finish with equal parts Scotch whisky and water [30 ml each], shake hard, strain into the glass and serve.

One of Mr Fouquet's creations. The pineapple rounds off the Scotch delicately.

### N°85   WHISKEY CRUSTA
#### YELLOW GLASS E

Place some ice cubes in a silver goblet, add 1 mouth spoon [10 ml] of gomme syrup, 2 dashes of orange bitters, 2 dashes of lemon juice, 4 dashes of maraschino, finish with [60 ml] Scotch whisky, shake well, strain into the glass that was rimmed with sugar beforehand, by slightly coating the glass with lemon juice and then sugar, and serve.

This one is on the sweet side. You might want to increase the lemon juice to a full barspoon or add a large lemon peel as a garnish, to get a better balance.

### N°86   WHISKEY DAISY L'AMOUR
#### CLEAR GLASS C

Place some ice cubes in a silver goblet, add 1 small spoon [flat barspoon] of powdered sugar, 2 mouth spoons [20 ml] of lemon juice, 4 dashes of raspberry syrup, finish with [45 ml] Scotch whisky and a squirt of siphon, shake well, strain into the glass and serve.

Dry yet as tart as a daisy should be. It is surprising that the hints of raspberry and Scotch do not conflict. A full barspoon of sugar will assist the balance.

## N° 87   WHISKEY FLIP
### CLEAR C GLASS

Place some ice cubes in a silver goblet, add 3 dashes of curaçao, 3 dashes of crème de noyaux, 1 fresh egg yolk, 1 spoon [1 barspoon] of powdered sugar, finish with [60 ml] Scotch or Irish whisky, shake hard, strain into the glass then sprinkle a little nutmeg on top and serve.

THIRD PART

# COBBLERS, PUNCHES, ETC.

AND

How to prepare them

THIRD PART

# COBBLERS, PUNCHES, ETC.

Cobblers and punches require great care in their preparation. The cobbler is a very popular beverage in America, and very fashionable during the summer. The cobbler can be made with sherry, whisky, brandy, champagne, etc. Like any other drinks, it is to the Americans that we owe those precious mixtures which are now enjoyed and sought out in hot climates. Their preparation requires great care to flatter the palate and the eyes. It's necessary to apply a special grace to garnish the glasses. Almost all cobblers and punches are fundamentally the same and vary from each other by the liquor they are made of. The base essences are almost always similar.

In season, garnish the glasses with the most fragrant fruits as much as possible, and replace them during the winter with pineapple and fruits preserved in eau-de-vie.

In this chapter you will also find all the fresh drinks such as citronade, orangeade, etc.

All those beverages are prepared directly in the glasses and served without need of the silver goblet for mixing.

However, some of my recipes exempt the rule.

It is good to use an ice strainer, to strain the ice for the people who do not like to drink from a straw.

This part introduces "cap shaking": a new technique within the book that is used to prepare iced coffee and tea drinks, enhancing the foam at the top of the glass. This was simply covering the glass with a metal cup and shaking. His advice after any cap shake is to rest the drink for a few minutes before serving to allow the foam settle. A few minutes actually means a few seconds, otherwise the drink will get too much dilution.

The drinks are a bit all over the place with more American and English libations than French ones. The slings are similar to collins. punches lack citrus and ornaments. Smashes have no mint. Temperance and less-temperate drinks with a few of Louis' concoctions, but not many.

Louis had his way of doing things and we have to respect that as his style.

**Passoire à boisson**
Pièce **18** fr.

# USTENSILES A PILER LA GLACE
## POUR COBBLERS & PUNCHS

Seau pour la Glace à rafraichir

| Petit... | Haut 0m10 | Pièce 14 fr. |
|---|---|---|
| Moyen.. | » 0m12 | » 17 » |
| Grand.. | » 0m14 | » 42 » |

**Pelle pour la Glace**
Pièce. ........ 6 fr.

**Machine à casser la glace** (nickelée)
Pièce...... **50 fr.**

**Passoire à boisson**
Pièce... **18 fr.**

**Couteau pique-glace**
Pièce **5 fr.**

## N°88   AMERICAN LEMONADE
### GLASS B

Fill the B glass with crushed ice, add 2 coffee spoons [2 barspoons] of powdered sugar, the juice of a lemon [20 ml], fill up with seltzer water, mix well, garnish with a lemon slice and straws, pour a few drops of ruby Port without mixing and serve.

Classic lemonade with a hint of port for colour and complexity.

## N°89   ALE PUNCH
### GLASS B

Fill half of the B glass with crushed ice, add the juice of a half a lemon [15 ml], pour in some pale ale, white wine and Curlier cognac in equal quantities [30 ml each], mix well, and at serving time sprinkle some nutmeg and garnish with 2 lemon zest, straws.

A very unusual drink. It just needs an extra barspoon of powdered sugar for balance. The white wine brings a vegetal freshness, the cognac a mellow ageing character and the pale ale a very pleasant earthy bitterness.

## N°90   BRANDY SLING
### GLASS B

Fill the B glass with crushed ice, add 2 spoons [2 barspoons] of powdered sugar, the juice of a lemon [30 ml], 1 Madeira glass [60 ml] of Curlier cognac, finish with seltzer water, mix well, straws and serve.

A really well-balanced drink. Essentially it is a Brandy Collins.

## N°91   BRANDY PUNCH
### GLASS B

Fill the B glass with crushed ice, add 1 small spoon [flat barspoon] of powdered sugar, 3 dashes of  Angostura, 4 dashes of curaçao, 2 dashes of noyaux, fill up with old cognac [60 ml], mix well, garnish with a lemon zest, add straws and serve.

This one is similar to the N° 5 Brandy Cocktail with the addition of sugar and served over crushed ice.

## N°92 BRANDY SMASH
### GLASS B

Fill the B glass with crushed ice, add 1 small spoon [flat barspoon] of powdered sugar, 4 dashes of curaçao, 4 dashes of noyaux, finish with Curlier cognac and water in equal quantities [30 ml each], mix well and sprinkle with nutmeg, add straws and serve.

More like a sangaree than a smash, this drink has a subtle up front sweetness that carries all the flavours through to the finish.

## N°93   BRANDY COBBLER
### GLASS B

Fill the B glass with crushed ice, add 2 coffee spoons [2 barspoons] of powdered sugar, 3 dashes of curaçao, 3 dashes of noyaux, fill up with [60 ml] Curlier cognac, mix well, insert an orange slice and a lemon slice down the inside of the glass, garnish with some fresh fruits or cherries preserved in eau-de-vie, straws, a few drops of ruby port without mixing and serve.

## N°94   BRUNSWICK COOLER
### GLASS A

Fill up the A glass with crushed ice, add the juice of a lemon [30 ml], 2 mouth spoons [4 barspoons] of powdered sugar, add a bottle of ginger ale, mix well, garnish with a lemon slice and some fruit, add straws and serve.

A sherberty ginger lemonade, the size of the glass is very relevant especially with this cocktail as the sugar content would be overpowering in a smaller vessel.

## N°95   BITTER HAVRAIS
### GLASS B

In the glass add a liqueur glass [30 ml] of cognac, then the bitters, crush a sugar cube at the bottom of the glass with a pestled spoon. Fill up with seltzer water, mix well.

Bitter Havrais is a forgotten bitters from Le Havre on the northwest coast in Haut-Normandie where the Seine terminates. The bitters was sold as far away as Australia in the 19th century.

## N°96   CRITERION LEMONADE
### GLASS B

Fill the B glass with crushed ice, add 3 spoons [3 barspoons] of powdered sugar, the juice of a half lemon [15 ml], 1 mouth spoon [10 ml] of raspberry syrup, finish with water [60 ml], mix well, garnish with a lemon slice, some fruit, straws, 1 dash of Sandeman Ruby Port without mixing and serve.

A richer version of N° 88, American Lemonade, the port and raspberry add up to a more complex alternative.

### N°97   CHAMPAGNE CUP
#### GLASS B

Fill the B glass with crushed ice, add 3 dashes of curaçao, 2 dashes of noyaux, 1 coffee spoon [5 ml] of maraschino, finish with American taste Henriot champagne, mix well, straws, when serving pour carefully a few drops of cherry brandy without mixing.

"American taste" champagne is a sweeter style that gives great body in this cup, especially served on crushed ice. There are lots of different cherry notes in the drink, with a hint of nutty orange in the background.

### N°98   CLARET CUP
#### GLASS B

Fill the B glass with crushed ice, add 2 coffee spoons [2 barspoons] of powdered sugar, 3 dashes of curaçao, 3 dashes of noyaux, 1 coffee spoon [1 barspoon] of maraschino, juice of half a lemon [15 ml], finish with some old Bordeaux red wine [60 ml], mix well, garnish with an orange slice, straws and serve.

Here is a really well-structured drink, all the ingredients layer nicely into a full bodied refreshing cup.

### N°99   LOUIS' CLARET CUP
#### GLASS B

Fill the B glass with crushed ice, add 1 coffee spoon [1 barspoon] of powdered sugar, 2 dashes of curaçao, 2 dashes of noyaux, half a liqueur glass [15 ml] of old kirsch, finish with a good red Bordeaux and Henriot Sillery suave champagne [45 ml each], mix well, garnish with an orange slice, straws and serve.

Dry and tannic, the kirsch adds a pungent cherry flavour lifting the other ingredients.

### N° 100    CRITERION REFRESHER
#### GLASS B

Fill the B glass with crushed ice, add 3 dashes of  Angostura, finish with half Turin vermouth, and half old gin [45 ml each], mix well, garnish with one lemon slice, straws and serve.

> Aged oude genever carries much better in this drink than unaged. Despite the name, this drink is quite intense and aromatic rather than refreshing.

### N° 101    CHICAGO
#### GLASS B

Fill the B glass with crushed ice, add 3 dashes of noyaux, 1 mouth spoon [10 ml] of grenadine, 1 liqueur glass [ 30 ml] of Curlier cognac, finish with half Amer Besset and half seltzer water, mix well, garnish with a lemon slice and serve with a straw.

> Amer Besset, presumably from the Midi-Pyrenees village of Besset, was classed with other "yellow fairy" (*la fée jaune*) gentian bitters such as Suze, Amer Picon and Salers.

### N° 102    CHAMPAGNE COBBLER
#### GLASS B

Fill the B glass with crushed ice, add 3 dashes of curaçao, 3 dashes of crème de noyaux, finish with Henriot Sillery suave champagne, mix well, garnish with an orange slice and a lemon slice, some seasonal fruit, straws, 2 dashes of Sandeman Ruby Port without mixing and serve.

> A little sugar would be a slight improvement.

### N°103   CLARET PUNCH
#### GLASS B

Fill the B glass with crushed ice, add 3 dashes of curaçao, 3 dashes of crème de noyaux, 2 spoons [2 barspoons] of powdered sugar, finish with some vintage red Bordeaux wine [60 ml], mix well, garnish with an orange slice, straws and serve.

### N°104   COFFEE PUNCH
#### GLASS B

Fill the B glass with crushed ice, add 2 dashes of curaçao, 2 dashes of noyaux, 2 spoons [2 barspoons] of powdered sugar, 1 liqueur glass [30 ml] of Curlier cognac, rum or kirsch depending of the person's taste, finish with coffee, mix well, straws and serve.

All the variants work well. My favourite uses rum, as it has more power and flavour than the others. The kirsch is pretty unusual. Nice but perhaps an acquired taste. And the cognac is too easy-going for my liking.

### N°105   CRITERION'S OWN PUNCH
#### GLASS B

Fill half of the B glass with crushed ice, add 2 dashes of curaçao, 2 dashes of noyaux, 2 spoons [2 barspoons] of powdered sugar, 1 fresh egg yolk, finish with coffee [60 ml], shake it up and down after affixing a silver goblet on your glass, wait a few minutes, uncover slowly to keep the foam in the glass, add straws and serve.

Similar to the Coffee Punch (listed above) without the booze in it. A great iced coffee with a lot of texture and a hint of fragrant nutty orange. A combination of both drinks, adding rum, kirsch or cognac to this one, is amazing.

### N° 106    CURACAO PUNCH
#### GLASS B

Fill the B glass with crushed ice, add 2 spoons [2 barspoons] of powdered sugar, half a lemon [15 ml] squeezed, 1 liqueur glass [30 ml] of Curlier cognac, 1 liqueur glass [30 ml] of rum, 1 Madeira glass [60 ml] of curaçao, finish with water [30 ml], mix well, garnish with an orange slice, some seasonal fruit, add straws and serve.

The recipe listed above is far too sweet and alcoholic. I had to cut down the curaçao to 30 ml. Even so, the drink is still quiet pungent but flavoursome and better balanced.

### N° 107    CANADIEN PUNCH
#### GLASS B

Fill the B glass with crushed ice, add 2 spoons [2 barspoons] of powdered sugar, 3 dashes of curaçao, 3 dashes of noyaux, 1 liqueur glass [30 ml] of rum, 1 mouth spoon [10 ml] of lemon juice, finish with water and rye whiskey in equal quantity [15 ml each], mix well, garnish with a lemon slice, and a pineapple chunk, straws and serve.

A sherberty punch. The rum and rye almost act like a *pain d'épice*, if you know what I mean.

### N° 108    COSMOPOLITAN CLARET PUNCH
#### GLASS B

Fill the B glass with crushed ice, add 3 dashes of curaçao, 2 dashes of noyaux, 2 spoons [2 barspoons] of powdered sugar, 1 liqueur glass [30 ml] of Curlier cognac. Fill up and finish with some red Bordeaux wine [45 ml], garnish with an orange slice, some seasonal fruits, straws and serve.

### N° 109    CIDER PUNCH
#### GLASS B

Fill the B glass with crushed ice, add 2 spoons [2 barspoons] of powdered sugar, 1 Madeira glass [60 ml] of dry sherry, 1 liqueur glass [30 ml] of Curlier cognac, juice of half a lemon [15 ml], finish with cider, mix well, garnish with an orange slice and 2 lemon zests, some seasonal fruits, straws and serve.

Loads of Americans are making Cider Punch with cognac, in which they macerate some cucumber peels for a few days, to give it a delicate and interesting perfume.

> A medium-sweet cider is necessary to balance the dry sherry and highlight the cognac. American readers should note: Cider in this recipe is the alcoholic cider that is traditional throughout Europe.

### N° 110    CIDER CUP
#### GLASS B

Fill the B glass with crushed ice, add 3 dashes of curaçao, 3 dashes of noyaux, 1 coffee spoon [1 barspoon] of powdered sugar, finish with a good cider and Henriot champagne in equal quantities [45 ml each], mix well, garnish with an orange slice, some seasonal fruits, straws and serve.

> Simply delicious. Cider and champagne are ideal together. Again, medium-sweet cider will work best.

### N° 111    CALIFORNIA WINE COBBLER
#### GLASS B

Fill the B glass with crushed ice, add 2 dashes of curaçao, 1 spoon [1 barspoon] of powdered sugar, the juice of an orange [60 ml], fill up

with some California wine [60 ml], mix well, 2 dashes of Sandeman
Ruby Port without mixing, straws and serve.

*Mild and easy. California white wine and orange juice will bring up
some fresh ripe peach flavours.*

### N° 112   EGG NOG
#### GLASS B

Fill half of the B glass with crushed ice, add 2 dashes of noyaux,
2 dashes of curaçao, 2 spoons [2 barspoons] of powdered sugar, 1 fresh
egg yolk, finish with milk and Sandeman sherry in equal quantities
[60 ml], on the glass affix a silver goblet and shake well, add straws
and serve.

### N° 113   EGG LEMONADE
#### GLASS B

Fill half of the B glass with crushed ice, add the juice of half
lemon [15 ml], 1 spoon [1 barspoon] of powdered sugar, 1 fresh egg,
affix a silver goblet on the glass and shake well. Then fill up with
seltzer water or soda, mix, add straws and serve.

*A lovely, rich and creamy textured lemonade.*

### N° 114   FISHERMAN'S PRAYER
#### GLASS B

Fill the B glass with crushed ice, add 1 spoon [1 barspoon] of
powdered sugar, juice of half a lemon [15 ml], 1 liqueur glass [30 ml]
of raspberry syrup, 1 liqueur glass [30 ml] of good rum, finish with
water [30 ml], mix well, garnish with some seasonal fruits, add straws
and serve.

This drink—made according to the recipe—is far too sickly sweet for a modern palate. A barspoon of raspberry syrup will be enough to bring balance of flavour together.

## N°115   GIN SLING
### GLASS B

Fill the B glass with crushed ice, add 1 spoon [1 barspoon] of powdered sugar, 1 liqueur glass [30 ml] of old gin, 1 lemon [30 ml] squeezed. Fill up with water, mix well, straws and serve.

The malty flavours of an aged oude genever carry better in this drink, if you follow the proportions above.

## N°116   GIN AND MILK
### GLASS B

Fill the B glass with crushed ice, add 1 spoon [1 barspoon] of gomme syrup, 2 dashes of crème de noyaux, finish with gin and milk in equal quantities [45 ml each], add straws and serve.

A comfy drink. The noyaux adds a nutty fragrance which is a lovely combination with an unaged oude genever. You could even add a sprinkle of nutmeg if you like.

## N°117   GIN PUNCH
### GLASS B

Fill the B glass with crushed ice, add 2 dashes of crème de noyaux, 1 mouth spoon of raspberry syrup [2 barspoons], 2 spoons [2 barspoons] of powdered sugar, finish with gin and water in equal quantities [60 ml each], mix well, garnish with an orange slice, a pineapple chunk, straws and serve.

If you follow this recipe precisely, you will end up with a very sweet drink with overpowering raspberry flavour. After a few trials, what worked best was to bring down the raspberry syrup to one barspoon. If you are looking for adventure a little lemon juice will help the drink.

### N° 118    GLASGOW FLIP
#### GLASS A

Fill half of the A glass with crushed ice, add 1 fresh egg, the juice of a lemon [30 ml], 1 spoon [1 barspoon] of powdered sugar. Fill up with a bottle of ginger ale, mix well, add straws and serve.

A virgin flip?! Oh well. Tone down the lemon juice a little to get a better balance.

### N° 119    HORSE GUARDS' BISHOP
#### GLASS B

Fill the B glass with crushed ice, add 4 dashes of curaçao, finish with rum and Henriot Sillery superior champagne in equal quantities [45 ml each], mix well, add a thin spiral-cut lemon twist as a garnish, add straws and serve.

A very pungent drink. It needs a barspoon of sugar to make it more palatable. The lemon spiral adds a pleasant burst of freshness.

### N° 120    ICE CREAM SODA
#### B GLASS

Fill the B glass with crushed ice, add 2 dashes of noyaux, half a liqueur glass [15 ml] of kirsch, 1 liqueur glass [30 ml] of crème de vanille, finish with milk and seltzer water in equal quantities [30 ml each], mix well, add straws and serve.

The name—hence the drink—tastes pretty much like a cream soda with hint of cherry flavour in the background.

## N° 121    ICED COFFEE
### B GLASS

Fill the B glass with crushed ice, add 2 dashes of crème de noyaux, half a glass [30 ml] of Curlier cognac or rum depending on the customer's taste, fill up with coffee, 2 spoons [2 barspoons] of powdered sugar, affix a silver goblet on your glass and shake hard, wait a few minutes, add straws and serve with all the foam intact.

Very similar to N° 104 Coffee Punch without the curaçao touch.

## N° 122    ICED TEA
### GLASS B

Fill the B glass with crushed ice, add 2 dashes of crème de noyaux, half a liqueur glass [15 ml] of rum, 2 spoons [2 barspoons] of powdered sugar, finish with cold tea, affix a silver goblet on your glass and shake hard. Wait a few minutes, and serve with all the foam intact, garnish with 2 orange slices and straws.

English breakfast tea works really well. I had to increase the rum to 30 ml to extract the raw sugary flavour of it. More subtle and refreshing than the coffee based one, but this depends on the tastes of the individual of course.

# UTENSILS FOR LEMON BEVERAGES

Lemon squeezer (nickel plated); piece…….. 80fr.
Lemon squeezer (silver plated); piece….. 44fr.
Lemon squeezer (silver plated); piece 20fr.
AA mobile cup receives the lemon juice and drips it through the B opening.
Gutter model, piece 17 fr.

# USTENSILES POUR LES BOISSONS AU CITRON

**Presse-Citron**
(nickelé)

Pièce........ **80** fr.

**Presse-Citron** (argenté)
Pièce..... **44** fr.

**Presse à Citron** entièrement en métal
blanc (argenté)   Pièce **20** fr.

AA cuvette mobile recevant le jus du
citron qui s'écoule par l'ouverture B
Modèle à gouttière   Pièce **17** fr.

### N° 123    JOHN COLLINS
#### GLASS B

Fill the B glass with crushed ice, add 2 spoons [2 barspoons] of powdered sugar, juice of 1 lemon [30 ml], 1 liqueur glass [30 ml] of gin, finish with seltzer water or soda, mix well, garnish with 1 lemon wheel, add straws and serve.

A refreshing collins. It has too little gin for my liking, but that's only me. Double the gin if you feel like it. I did.

### N° 124    LEMON AND DASH
#### GLASS A

Place one ice chunk in the A glass, pour half full of fizzy lemonade, fill up with Allsopp's pale ale, garnish with 1 lemon zest and serve.

In other words, an old fashioned shandy that is as delicious as ever.

### N° 125    LEMON SQUASH
#### GLASS B

Fill the B glass with crushed ice, add 2 spoons [2 barspoons] of powdered sugar, 1 lemon [30 ml] squeezed, finish with seltzer water or soda, mix well, garnish with a lemon slice, add straws and serve.

Classic fresh lemonade.

### N° 126    MILK PUNCH
#### GLASS B

Fill the B glass with ice cubes, add 2 dashes of noyaux, 2 spoons [2 barspoons] of powdered sugar, half a liqueur glass [15 ml] of Curlier cognac, half a liqueur glass [15 ml] of rum, finish with milk [60 ml], adjust a silver goblet on your glass and shake hard. Wait a few minutes, and serve with all the foam, sprinkle with nutmeg, add straws and serve.

> The flavours are nicely integrated and the milk gives it a silky texture.

## N°127   MOTHER'S MILK
### GLASS B

Fill the B glass with crushed ice, add 4 dashes of curaçao, 2 dashes of noyaux, 1 mouth spoon [10 ml] of grenadine, 1 fresh egg yolk, 1 liqueur glass [30 ml] of Curlier cognac, finish with milk [30 ml], affix a silver goblet on your glass and shake hard. Wait a few minutes, and serve with all the foam, straws, sprinkle with nutmeg.

> Modern store-bought grenadine destroys the flavours of curaçao and noyaux. Pomegranate syrup is a better choice for this drink. It also complements the cognac and diary products transforming this into a mouth-filling sweetish milky drink.

## N°128   MISSISSIPI [sic] PUNCH
### GLASS B

Fill the B glass with crushed ice, add 2 spoons [2 barspoons] of powdered sugar, 3 dashes of lemon juice, 1 liqueur glass [30 ml] of rum, 1 liqueur glass [30 ml] of Curlier cognac, 1 liqueur glass [30 ml] of bourbon whiskey, finish with seltzer water, mix well, garnish with some seasonal fruits, a lemon slice, add straws and serve.

> One of those challenging concoctions, there is far too much booze (as you can imagine). Bring each spirit to 20 ml for a more palatable drink. The idea of blending these three aged spirits is really good as each of them brings their own character to the mix.

## N° 129    ORANGEADE
### GLASS B

Fill the B glass with crushed ice, add 2 spoons [2 barspoons] of powdered sugar, 1 liqueur glass [30 ml] of curaçao, the juice of 1 orange [60 ml], finish with water [30 ml], mix well, garnish with an orange slice, add straws and serve.

> Orange squash would be a perfect translation to the taste of this drink. Depending of the type of orange you are using the orangeade will change. Sour oranges work better.

## N° 130    ORGEAT LEMONADE
### GLASS B

Fill the B glass with crushed ice, add 1 spoon [1 barspoon] of powdered sugar, juice of half a lemon [15 ml], 1 liqueur glass [30 ml] of orgeat syrup, finish with water [60 ml], mix well, garnish with 1 lemon slice, some seasonal fruits, straws, 4 dashes of raspberry syrup and serve without mixing.

## N° 131    ORGEAT PUNCH
### GLASS B

Fill the B glass with crushed ice, add 2 dashes of crème de noyaux, 1 liqueur glass [30 ml] of Curlier cognac, finish with orgeat and water, mix well, garnish with 1 lemon slice, some seasonal fruits, straws and 2 dashes of ruby Port before serving.

> I cannot work this one out as listed. The flavour intensity of my ingredients is probably far from what Louis' were at the time. So, I kept the noyaux and the ruby Port as it is mentioned, doubled the cognac [60 ml], cut the orgeat to 2 barspoons and added 60 ml of water. The result was a long almond and cognac drink with a hint of tannin.

## N° 132    OLD CHUM'S REVIVER
### GLASS B

Fill the B glass with crushed ice, add the juice of half a lemon [15 ml], 1 spoon [1 barspoon] of powdered sugar, 1 liqueur glass [30 ml] of Curlier cognac, finish with strawberry syrup [10 ml] and seltzer water [30 ml], or soda, mix well, garnish with cherries preserved in eau-de-vie, add straws and serve.

## N° 133    PORT SANGAREE
### GLASS B

Fill the B glass with crushed ice, add 2 dashes of curaçao, 1 spoon [1 barspoon] of powdered sugar, finish with Sandeman Ruby Port and water in equal quantities [60 ml each], mix well, sprinkle with nutmeg, add straws and serve.

## N° 134    PRINCE OF WALES
### GLASS B

Fill the B glass with crushed ice, add 3 dashes of curaçao, 2 dashes of noyaux, 1 Madeira glass [60 ml] of dry Madeira, 1 spoon [1 barspoon] of powdered sugar, finish with Henriot dry champagne and seltzer water [30 ml each], mix well, garnish with 1 lemon slice, straws, top with 2 dashes of cherry brandy and serve without mixing.

A very subtle, winey drink, just delicious, silky and refreshing.

## N° 135    PUNCH A LA ROMAINE
### GLASS B

Fill the B glass with crushed ice, add 4 dashes of curaçao, 1 spoon [1 barspoon] of powdered sugar, 2 dashes of lemon juice, 1 fresh egg, 1 coffee spoon of aged rum [5 ml], finish with some white Bordeaux wine [60 ml], affix a silver goblet on your glass and shake hard, add straws, sprinkle with nutmeg and serve.

A nice grassy and herbaceous sauvignon combines with the hint aged rum to make an amazing punch.

### N°136    PHILADELPHIA BOATING PUNCH
#### GLASS B

Fill the B glass with crushed ice, add 2 spoons [2 barspoons] of powdered sugar, juice of a half lemon, 1 liqueur glass [30 ml] of rum, 1 liqueur glass [30 ml] of Curlier cognac, finish with water, mix well, garnish with some seasonal fruits, a lemon slice, add straws and serve.

### N°137    RUM COLD PUNCH
#### GLASS B

Fill the B glass with crushed ice, add 3 dashes of curaçao, 3 dashes of noyaux, 2 spoons [2 barspoons] of powdered sugar, finish with old rum and water [60 ml each], mix well, sprinkle with nutmeg, straws and serve.

### N°138    RANSOM COOLER
#### GLASS B

Fill the B glass with crushed ice, add 3 dashes of noyaux, 4 dashes of curaçao, 1 mouth spoon [10 ml] of grenadine, 1 mouth spoon [10 ml] of old kirsch, finish with half bitter and half seltzer water [30 ml each], mix well, garnish with 1 lemon slice, straws and serve.

Bitter? What bitter?! I just went for equal measures of Amer Picon and water, and it worked really well with the kirsch and grenadine. Despite the similar name, this drink bears no resemblance to the Remsen Cooler.

## N° 139   ROCKY MOUNTAIN PUNCH
### GLASS B

Fill the B glass with crushed ice, add 2 spoons [2 barspoons] of powdered sugar, juice of half a lemon [15 ml], half a glass of Jamaican rum [15 ml], 1 mouth spoon [10 ml] of maraschino, finish with Henriot champagne American taste, mix well, garnish with 1 lemon slice and some seasonal fruits, 1 piece of sugar candy, add straws and serve.

Dry and zesty overall. Maraschino, rum and champagne can't really go wrong together. For more information about "American taste" champagne see N° 97 Champagne Cup.

## N° 140   ROMAN PUNCH
### GLASS B

Fill the B glass with crushed ice, add 1 coffee spoon [1 barspoon] of powdered sugar, 3 dashes of lemon juice, 1 orange squeezed [60 ml], 1 liqueur glass of curaçao [30 ml], 1.5 liqueur glasses of old rum [45 ml], finish with cognac, mix well, seasonal fruits, add straws, top with 2 dashes of Sandeman Ruby Port without mixing and serve.

A burst of orange. A 40% curaçao is essential to complement the rum and cognac while keeping the sweetness level low.

## UTENSILS TO OPEN WINE BOTTLES

Mechanical bottle opener (small); piece................. 30fr.
Large bottle opener (nickel plated); piece..... 80 fr.

# USTENSILES POUR LE DÉBOUCHAGE DES BOUTEILLES

**Tire-Bouchon** mécanique
(petit)

Pièce................ **30 fr.**

**Grand Tire-Bouchon** (nickelé)

Pièce..... **80 fr.**

### N° 141    RHINE WINE COBBLER
#### GLASS B

Fill the B glass with crushed ice, add 1 coffee spoon [1 barspoon] of powdered sugar, 3 dashes of curaçao, 2 dashes of noyaux, finish with Rhine wine and water in equal quantities [45 ml each], mix well, garnish with some seasonal fruits, 1 pineapple chunk, 1 orange slice, add straws and serve.

N. B. – This beverage is very trendy in Germany.

Sweet Riesling holds better with the amount of crushed ice and water.

### N° 142    ROCKY MOUNTAIN COOLER
#### GLASS B

Fill half of the B glass with crushed ice, add 1 fresh egg, 1 spoon [1 barspoon] of powdered sugar, juice of a lemon [30 ml], finish with some good cider, shake well by affixing a silver goblet on the glass, add straws, sprinkle some nutmeg and serve.

This can work by adding more sugar in it. Even using a medium sweet cider, the drink still is a tiny bit sour. American readers should note: The cider is, of course, European fermented and filtered cider.

### N° 143    SHERRY SANGAREE
#### GLASS B

Fill the B glass with crushed ice, 3 dashes of curaçao, 2 dashes of noyaux, 1 spoon [1 barspoon] of powdered sugar and finish with Sandeman sherry [60 ml], mix well, add straws, sprinkle with nutmeg and serve.

### N° 144    SOYER AU CHAMPAGNE
#### GLASS B

Fill the B glass with crushed ice, add 3 dashes of curaçao, half a liqueur glass [15 ml] of maraschino, fill up with champagne Jules Mumm dry, mix well, add straws, and at the serving time pour without mixing a few drops of good crème de vanille.

> Clean with a dry sensation overall. This recipe was popularized by Jerry Thomas but was created by Alexis Benoit Soyer, a French chef who escaped the revolution and moved to London where he became the most highly paid chef in the world. I recommend the book *Relish: The Extraordinary Life* of Alexis Soyer.

### N° 145    SHERRY COBBLER
#### GLASS B

Fill the B glass with crushed ice, add 2 dashes of noyaux, 2 dashes of curaçao, 2 coffee spoons [2 barspoons] of powdered sugar, finish with Sandeman sherry [60 ml], mix well, garnish with an orange and a lemon wheel, some seasonal fruits, add straws and at serving time, slowly pour a little Ruby Port without mixing.

### N° 146    SANTA CRUZ PUNCH
#### GLASS B

Fill the B glass with crushed ice, add 2 dashes of curaçao, 2 dashes of noyaux, 1 spoon [1 barspoon] of powdered sugar, finish with old rum and water [60 ml each], mix well, garnish with a lemon slice and serve.

### N° 147    SARATOGA COOLER
#### GLASS A

Fill half of the A glass with crushed ice, 1 spoon of powdered sugar, juice of half a lemon [15 ml], a bottle of ginger ale, mix well, add straws and serve.

A more intense ginger version of the Brunswick Cooler.

### N° 148    SAUTERNE PUNCH
#### GLASS B

Fill the B glass with crushed ice, add 1 spoon [1 barspoon] of powdered sugar, 3 dashes of curaçao, finish with [80 ml] some Sauternes wine (Château Peyron), mix well, garnish with 1 orange slice, 1 lemon slice, half a pineapple slice, some straws seasonal fruits and serve.

Made in a similar fashion to many wine punches of the time, port and sherry included. The sauterne is definitely my favourite out there for its round honey, citrus and floral notes.

### N° 149    STONE FENCE
#### GLASS B

Fill the B glass with crushed ice, add 3 dashes of gomme syrup, 1 liqueur glass [30 ml] of Curlier cognac, fill up with soft cider, mix well, straws and serve.

Cognac seems to be the original spirit, though some bartenders advised an optional apple jack instead of cognac. Medium cider works better in the recipe above. See also the Whiskey variation below (N° 157).

### N° 150    TIP-TOP PUNCH
#### GLASS B

Fill the B glass with crushed ice, add juice of half a lemon [15 ml], 1 liqueur glass [30 ml] of good Curlier cognac, fill up with Henriot white label champagne, mix well, garnish with an orange slice, a pineapple chunk, some seasonal fruits, straws and serve.

Most Tip-Top Punch recipes calls for cognac but some of them use orange curaçao instead. Louis' is dry and sour. A barspoon of powdered sugar will bring up the flavours together.

### N° 151    VANILLA PUNCH
#### GLASS B

Fill the B glass with crushed ice, add 2 dashes of curaçao, 2 dashes of noyaux, equal quantities of crème de vanille and water [60 ml each], mix well, garnish with an orange slice, add straws and serve.

This one came about around the mid-1850s. Most of the recipes calling for it, include lemon juice but also cognac. Some recipes infuse a vanilla bean in it or add vanilla essences and other use a little soda instead of water.

Louis' recipe is more a vanillin water.

### N° 152    WHISKEY SLING
#### B GLASS

Fill the B glass with crushed ice, add 2 spoons [2 barspoons] of powdered sugar, 1 squeezed lemon [30 ml], 1 liqueur glass of Scotch whisky [30 ml], finish with seltzer water or soda, mix well, add straws and serve.

**CUILLÈRE A PILON**

pour Juleps, Bitter Havrais, etc.

## Nº 153   WHISKEY WHITE FLUSH
### B GLASS

Fill the B glass with crushed ice, add 2 dashes of curaçao, pour in equal quantities of milk and rye whiskey [60 ml each], mix well, add straws and serve.

I guess Louis meant to title this one a "Whiskey White Plush". Originally an American drink consisting of a glass of milk served along with a bottle of whiskey that is handed to the customer to help themselves. Apparently it was first served in general stores to mask the alcohol within the drink in order to abuse a country man's naivety, getting him drunk before he placed his dry goods order back in the first quarter of the 19th century. It is not a great concoction when made with modern homogenised milk. Add sugar and it becomes a more palatable Milk Punch.

## Nº 154   WHISKEY SMASH
### GLASS B

Fill the B glass with crushed ice, add 2 dashes of curaçao, 2 dashes of noyaux, 2 spoons [2 barspoons] of powdered sugar, finish with [60 ml] whisky (Scotch or Irish), mix well, add straws and serve.

## Nº 155   WHISKEY COBBLER
### GLASS B

Fill the B glass with crushed ice, add 2 dashes of curaçao, 2 dashes of noyaux, 2 coffee spoons [1 barspoon] of powdered sugar, finish with [60 ml] whisky (Scotch or Irish), mix well, garnish with an orange slice and a lemon slice, some seasonal fruits, straws and at serving time pour slowly a little Sandeman Ruby Port without mixing.

### N° 156    WHISKEY SNAPPER
#### GLASS B

Fill the B glass with crushed ice, add 1 spoon [1 barspoon] of powdered sugar, 4 dashes of lemon juice, 2 dashes of raspberry syrup, 1 liqueur glass of Scotch whisky [30 ml], 1 small spoon of honey [flat barspoon], finish with seltzer water or soda, mix well, garnish with a lemon zest, add straws and serve.

> Whiskey Snapper is an unusual drink. It is also very rare. It was not mentioned in any other publication around that time. The closest—a Brandy Snapper,—is listed in Franck Newman's 1904 book. I believe this is one of Louis' original recipes, and a rather good one: Honeyed raspberry with a sparkle of lemon seals the Scotch nicely. A full barspoon of honey water (equal parts honey and water) will improve mixability.

### N° 157    WHISKEY STONE FENCE
#### GLASS B

Fill the B glass with crushed ice, add 2 spoons [2 barspoons] of powdered sugar, 3 dashes of gomme syrup, 1 glass of Scotch or Irish whisky, finish with cider, mix well, straws and serve.

> As this drink is usually made with sweet cider and no sugar, dry cider works better with the added sweetness in Louis' formula.

### N° 158    WHISKEY FIX
#### GLASS B

Fill the B glass with crushed ice, 2 spoons [2 barspoons] of powdered sugar, 3 dashes of lemon juice, 1 liqueur glass [30 ml] of Scotch whisky, 1.5 glasses of pineapple syrup, garnish with some seasonal fruits, add straws and serve.

Pineapple syrup is the classic ingredient for making fixes. Some bartenders also add lemon rind within the mix, to gain the bitterness of the oil. Louis' adaptation is far too sweet. You want to drop the sugar completely and level the pineapple syrup to 10 ml.

## N° 159   WHISKEY PUNCH FROID
### B GLASS

Fill the B glass with crushed ice, add 3 dashes of curaçao, 3 dashes of noyaux, 1 spoon [1 barspoon] of powdered sugar, finish with some [60 ml] Scotch or Irish whisky, mix well, add straws and serve.

A lemon twist does well in this punch.

FOURTH PART

# SUMMER DRINKS

AND

HOW TO PREPARE THEM

FOURTH PART

# SUMMER DRINKS

Summer drinks can only be served during the good season, because of the fresh fruits and herbs that we must employ for their preparation.

Amongst these drinks, those which require the most attention and care are the juleps, that is to say all the drinks made from fresh peppermint, which we muddle with a spoon fitted out with a pestle along with a little sugar and alcohol to extract the entire aroma.

The Mint Julep is a beverage most in vogue in America and the Americans enjoy them mostly during the hot season.

The preparation requires a very particular refinement and the garnish, before serving, demands a certain sense of taste to prepare.

Because of the colour that we obtain when preparing the juleps, we will take the red glasses by preference to mask the colour and flatter the palate. The glasses need a very thick base to withstand the shocks of the spoon when muddling.

For the strawberry and raspberry punches, it is necessary to shake them heavily in silver cups with big chunks of ice, to crush the fruit more easily while extracting the perfume.

For fruity drinks it will be preferable to use a drink strainer (page 26) in order to extract the last drop of juice that the fruit must give.

This section is principally about juleps with a few smashes and punches served up. As you will discover, Louis Fouquet has a very particular and meticulous way of making Juleps. He uses yellow Chartreuse as a base and complements it with other spirits. I really like the fact that Louis refreshes the mint by soaking it in lemon juice before using it as a garnish to add a subtle citrus aroma to the drink. However, he still includes sugar in it, which I found far too sweet. You might want skip the sugar in all of them to get a less candy-like drink.

Chartreuse liqueur, green or yellow, is normally used as a modifier to mixed drinks and both of them work amazingly well with mint. Rum, gin, brandy and whiskey are used within the drinks and also as a drizzle to complement the finish as Professor Jerry Thomas used to do. I think Louis' finishing is much cleverer than the Professor's as he enhances each spirit with an alternative from the same category.

I believe he was a pioneer in this method as none of his contemporaries or predecessors were using sweet, honeyed herbal liqueur in their juleps. It was soon picked up by Charlie Paul of the Royal Aquarium in London, who also worked in Paris and New York and published his *Recipes of American and Other Iced Drinks* in 1902. Did Charlie and Louis have a passing meeting in Paris or even bartend together? Well, we may never know for sure.

### N° 160   BRANDY JULEP
#### RED GLASS B

In the glass, muddle 3-4 fresh mint leaves with 1 spoon [barspoon] of powdered sugar, then add 1 liqueur glass [30 ml] of Curlier cognac, fill up with crushed ice, 1 liqueur glass [30 ml] of yellow Chartreuse, finish with water and mix well, soak a mint stalk in lemon juice, place it in the middle of the glass, add straws, garnish with seasonal fruits, top with 2 dashes of good cognac without mixing, sprinkle the top with powdered sugar and serve.

### N° 161   CRITERION RUM SMASH
#### RED GLASS C

Place some ice chunks in a silver goblet and add 1 spoon [barspoon] of powdered sugar, 2 mint leaves, finish with [60 ml] rum and water [15 ml], shake well, strain into the glass, garnish with seasonal fruits, add straws and serve.

A great rum smash, perfectly well balanced especially with an aged rhum agricole.

### N° 162   CHAMPAGNE JULEP
#### RED GLASS B

In the glass, muddle 3-4 fresh mint stalks with 1 spoon [barspoon] of powdered sugar, then add 1 liqueur glass [30 ml] of Curlier cognac, fill up with crushed ice, add 1 liqueur glass [30 ml] of yellow Chartreuse, finish with Henriot dry champagne, and mix well, soak a mint stalk in lemon juice, place it in the middle of the glass, straws, seasonal fruits, 2 dashes of good rum without mixing, sprinkle with powdered sugar and serve.

### N° 163    FANCY WHISKEY SMASH
#### RED GLASS C

Place some ice chunks in a silver goblet and add 3 mint leaves, 1 spoon [barspoon] of powdered sugar, 1 Madeira glass [60 ml] whisky [Scotch or Irish] and finish with water [15 ml], shake well, strain into the glass, garnish with seasonal fruits, add straws and serve.

> I wonder why this smash is "fancier" than the rum version? The recipes are identical except for the base spirit.

### N° 164    GIN JULEP
#### RED GLASS B

In the glass, muddle 3-4 fresh mint stalks with 1 spoon [barspoon] of powdered sugar, then add 1 liqueur glass [30 ml] of old gin, fill up with crushed ice, 1 liqueur glass [30 ml] of yellow Chartreuse, finish with water and mix well, soak a mint stalk in lemon juice, place it in the middle of the glass, straws, garnish with seasonal fruits, top with 2 dashes of old tom gin without mixing, sprinkle with powdered sugar and serve.

### N° 165    KILRAIN PUNCH
#### RED GLASS E

Place some ice chunks in a silver goblet and add 3 mint sprigs, 1 spoon [barspoon] of powdered sugar, half a liqueur glass [15 ml] old rum, 2 spoons [10 ml] raspberry syrup, finish with [15 ml] water, shake well, strain into the glass, garnish with seasonal fruits and a mint sprig, add straws and serve.

> The quantity of rum in this drink does not seem right. Half a liqueur glass [15 ml] is almost undetectable against the other ingredients and the drink is far too sweet.
> I advise boosting the rum to 60 ml and leaving the sugar out of it!

### N° 166   MINT JULEP
#### RED GLASS B

In the glass, muddle 4 fresh mint stalks with 1 spoon [barspoon] of powdered sugar, then add 1 liqueur glass [30 ml] of Curlier cognac, fill up with crushed ice, 1 liqueur glass [30 ml] of yellow Chartreuse, finish with water and mix well, soak a mint stalk in lemon juice, place it in the middle of the glass, add 3 dashes of good rum without mixing, fruits, straws, sprinkle with powdered sugar and serve.

### N° 167   THE PINEAPPLE JULEP
#### RED GLASS B

In the glass, muddle 2-3 fresh mint sprigs, juice of an orange with 1 spoon [5 ml] of raspberry syrup, 1 spoon [5 ml] of maraschino, 1 spoon [5 ml] of gin, 1 liqueur glass [30 ml] of crème d'ananas, fill up with crushed ice. Finish with pineapple juice [30 ml], mix well, soak a mint stalk in lemon juice, place it in the middle of the glass, seasonal fruits, pineapple chunk, straws and serve.

> This julep is very different from any others listed in the book, and also very different from any other Pineapple Julep listed in any book. First of all it contains mint, and the gin is minimal. Crème d'ananas? What for?! I think the editor overlooked the proportions in this recipe. If you try it at home you will get sweet pineapple juice with hint of mint. I tried many different ways, turning it into an okay drink without changing much of the DNA. The best result came when I increased the gin to 30 ml and dropped the crème d'ananas.

### N° 168   RASPBERRY PUNCH
#### GREEN GLASS C

Place some ice chunks in a silver goblet and add a dozen ripe raspberries, a glass [50 ml] of cognac Curlier, 1 coffee spoon [5 ml] of maraschino, 1 coffee spoon [5 ml] of raspberry syrup, shake well, strain into the glass, fill with Henriot Sillery superior champagne, garnish with a raspberry, sprinkle with powdered sugar, straws and serve.

This drink is quite strong, but a delicious summer champagne punch.

### N° 169    RUM JULEP
#### RED GLASS B

It is done exactly like the Brandy Julep, with rum instead of the cognac Curlier.

### N° 170    STRAWBERRY PUNCH
#### GREEN GLASS C

Place some ice chunks in a silver goblet and add a dozen ripe strawberries, a glass [50 ml] of Curlier cognac, 1 coffee spoon [5 ml] of maraschino, 1 coffee spoon [5 ml] of strawberry syrup, shake well, strain into the glass, fill with Henriot Sillery superior champagne, garnish with a strawberry, sprinkle with powdered sugar, straws and serve.

### N° 171    WHISKEY JULEP
#### RED B GLASS

In the glass, muddle 3-4 fresh mint stalks with 1 spoon [barspoon] of powdered sugar, then add 1 liqueur glass [30 ml] of Scotch whisky, fill up with Scotch whisky, 1 liqueur glass [30 ml] of yellow chartreuse, finish with water and mix well, soak a mint stalk in lemon juice, place it in the middle of the glass, straws, garnish with seasonal fruits, 2 dashes of good rye whisky, sprinkle with powdered sugar and serve.

I guess there is an editing error in this one. Louis would not have omitted the crushed ice to replace it for another measure of Scotch. No way! Follow the recipe as it is with crushed ice instead of another measure of Scotch.

FIFTH PART

# WINTER DRINKS

AND

How to prepare them

FIFTH PART

# WINTER DRINKS

The American hot beverages are almost as original as the other cold, all are delicious and many are recommended by our most eminent doctors as sovereign against the strongest colds and bronchial diseases.

They need no special tools and their manufacture is so simple which makes them accessible to everyone.

At this time in France, among the most famous drink, I quote the Tom & Jerry, replacing the eggnog of our ancestors which is of an indisputable efficiency for delicate stomachs.

The port wine Negus is also very popular in America in high society salons and replaces many punches and hot grog of our social evening.

For the preparation of winter drinks, you should always make sure to rinse the glasses you must use with hot water, in order to prevent them from breaking from the strong heat of the drink you pour in, and always dissolve sugar in water before you pour any alcohol to be dissolved promptly.

For the service of a few drinks, it will be good to use some glass holders (page 125) of two sizes, in order to adjust the glasses B and C, to preserve the fingers of the high heat while drinking, and always have a few spices, cloves, cinnamon, etc..

Here is a section on old-timers. Most of these cheerful inventions appeared at the turn of the 19th century or long before, when ice was not available on every corner to mix drinks, and the lack of central heating made hot drinks very popular.

These are all very straight forward and therefore commentary would sound as gratuitous as a French 'VaVaVoom'. But just look up for Louis' adaptation of the Blue Blazer or the rum flip for innovation.

# THE

# CRITERION

AMERICAN ENGLISH

AND FRENCH DRINCKS

LUNCHEON BAR

121, Rue Saint-Lazare, 121

## PARIS

# SOUPERS

## UTENSILS FOR WINTER DRINKS & HOT DRINKS

Glass holder Mazagran
Plain model, strong rim piece 7 "
Up to day's model, " " " 7 "
Guilloche model, " " " 8 "

Porcelain Cup
Small….. piece 3fr. 25
Large….. piece 4fr. "

| WHITE METAL | | | Polished | Silver Plated | |
|---|---|---|---|---|---|
| 1 glass capacity piece | 13 | | " | 17 | " |
| 2 " " " | | | 16 | " | 19 | " |
| 3 " " " | | | 19 | " | 22 | " |
| 4 " " " | | | 22 | " | 26 | " |

Spices-Holder
3 shells (gold inside)
Piece… 35fr.

# USTENSILES POUR WINTER DRINKS
## BOISSONS CHAUDES

**Porte Verre Mazagran**

| | | | | |
|---|---|---|---|---|
| Modèle uni, bord fort | Pièce | 7 | » |
| " à jours | » | " | 7 | " |
| » guilloché | » | » | 8 | " |

**Tasse Porcelaine**

Petite . . . . . pièce **3 fr. 25**
Grande. . . . » **4 fr.** »

| MÉTAL BLANC | | | Avivé | Argenté |
|---|---|---|---|---|
| Contenance 1 verre | pièce | 13 » | 17 » |
| » 2 » | " | 16 » | 19 " |
| » 3 » | " | 19 » | 22 » |
| » 4 » | " | 22 » | 26 " |

**Porte-Épices**

3 coquilles (intérieur doré)

Pièce. . . **35 fr.**

8.

## N° 172   AMERICAN GROG
### CLEAR B GLASS

Heat up 1 mouth spoon [10 ml] of gomme syrup with old rum and water [100 ml each], mix well and pour into the glass, garnish with 1 lemon wheel spiked with 4 cloves, serve with a glass-holder.

*The American Grog was all ready popular in French café around the mid-1850s. Let the lemon wheel and cloves infuse in the drink before drinking.*

## N° 173   ALE FLIP
### B GLASS

Heat up glass [125 ml] of (allsopp's) pale ale, on the side, mix 1 egg with 1 mouth spoon [2 barspoons] of powdered sugar and sprinkle with nutmeg, beat well and pour in little quantity and slowly the beer while mixing briskly, then transfer back and forth from one vessel to another until a froth start to form, pour into the glass, serve with a glass-holder.

*This beverage is delicious at the onset of a bout with the flu.*

## N° 174   BRANDY PUNCH
### RED E GLASS

Heat up half Curlier fine champagne cognac and half water [40 ml each], 1 spoon [1 barspoon] of powdered sugar, pour into the glass and serve as it flamed.

## N° 175   BLUE BLAZES
### RED E GLASS

Mix 1 spoon [1 barspoon] of candy sugar, 1 spoon [1 barspoon] of good honey, finish with water and Scotch [40 ml each], heat up and transfer back and forth from one vessel to another the flamed liquid, to make a long blue flame trail and serve.

Well, he didn't call it the "Blue Blazer", so Louis has every right to sweeten it with candy sugar and honey as much as he wants.

Of course it is a take on Jerry Thomas' own creation, born when a gold prospector said to the professor, "Fix me up some hell-fire that'll shake me right down to my gizzard!"

Mr Fouquet's alternative is more interesting: It still makes a spectacular show and the honey brings a unique, complex and pleasant character when combined with the Scotch and moderated by the sugar

.

## N° 176   CRITERION PORT NEGUS
### RED E GLASS

1 spoon [1 barspoon] of gomme syrup, finish with Sandeman ruby port [80 ml], heat up and pour into the glass, garnish with one lemon slice spiked with 3 cloves and serve.

## N° 177   GIN TODDY
### C GLASS

Heat up gin, water [50 ml each], 1 spoon [1 barspoon] of powdered sugar, pour into the glass, serve with a glass-holder.

## N° 178   GIN CLING
### C GLASS

Heat up gin [50 ml], 1 spoon [1 barspoon] of lemon juice, finish with water [50 ml], 1 spoon of powdered sugar [1 barspoon], pour into the glass, serve with a glass-holder.

The word "Cling" is no mistake here. The drink was popular in France at the end of the 19th century onward and is also mentioned in Spanish editions at the beginning of the 20th century.

### N° 179   OLD FASHIONED HOT GIN SLING
#### GREEN E GLASS
Heat up 1 spoon [1 barspoon] of gomme syrup, water and gin [50 ml each], scrape a little nutmeg, pour into the glass and serve.

### N° 180   ITALIEN FLIP
#### GREEN E GLASS
Mix a fresh egg yolk, 1 spoon [1 barspoon] of powdered sugar, glass [50 ml] of Curlier fine de champagne cognac, finish with Marsala [50 ml], heat up while whisking hard, pour into the glass, sprinkle some nutmeg and serve.

### N° 181   JERSEY TODDY
#### B GLASS
Heat up 1 spoon [1 barspoon] of powdered sugar, 1 good glass [60 ml] of cider eau-de-vie, half apple oven cooked, finish with water [60 ml], pour into the glass, sprinkle some nutmeg and serve with a glass-holder.

This recipe was originally named the Apple Toddy in the *Bon Vivant Companion* by Jerry Thomas.

### N° 182   KIRSCH PUNCH
#### GREEN E GLASS
Heat up old kirsch, water [50 ml each], 1 spoon [1 barspoon] of powdered sugar, pour into the glass and serve as it flame.

### N° 183   MILK PUNCH
#### B GLASS
Heat up glass of good milk [125 ml], pour into the B glass rum and Curlier cognac, in equal quantity [50 ml each] from the right

hand, by whisking them from the left hand, sprinkle some nutmeg, serve with a glass-holder.

Two barspoons of sugar would definitely help matters in that one.

### N°184    RUM PUNCH
#### RED E GLASS

Heat up old rum and water in equal quantity [50 ml each] 1 spoon [1 barspoon] of powdered sugar, pour into the glass and serve.

### N°185    RUM FLIP
#### B GLASS

Heat up half glass [125 ml] of pale ale (allsopp's), on the side mix 1 fresh egg, 1 liqueur glass [30 ml] of good rum, sprinkle with nutmeg and ginger, beat well and heat up slowly, then transfer back and forth from one vessel to another until a froth start to form.

Even though you are using rum, it still needs an additional barspoon of sugar.

### N°186    SANDEMAN'S PORT NEGUS
#### RED C GLASS

Heat up 1 spoon [1 barspoon] of gomme, liqueur glass of cognac [15 ml], finish with [100 ml] Sandeman ruby port, garnish with 1 orange slice spiked with 3 cloves and serve.

### N°187    PORT SANGAREE (HOT)
#### C GLASS

Heat up water and Sandeman ruby port [50 ml each], 1 spoon [1 barspoon] of powdered sugar, sprinkle some nutmeg, pour, glass holder and serve.

### N° 188   PUNCH CUSENIER SEC
#### E GLASS

A glass [50 ml] of Cusenier punch, water [30 ml], liqueur glass [15 ml] rum, 1 spoon [1 barspoon] gomme syrup, heat up and serve

### N° 189   PUNCH DU 69ᴱ REGIMENT
#### C GLASS

Heat up liqueur glass [15 ml] of Irish whiskey, liqueur glass [15 ml] of Scotch whisky, 1 spoon [1 barspoon] of powder (meaning powdered sugar), 3 dashes of lemon juice, finish with [50 ml] water, pour into the glass, garnish with 1 lemon slice and serve with a glass-holder.

### N° 190   SLEEPER
#### RED E GLASS

Heat up a fresh egg yolk, 1 spoon [1 barspoon] of lemon juice, 1 spoon [1 barspoon] powdered sugar, 2 cloves, 1 piece of cinnamon, finish with rum and water [40 ml each], pour into the glass and serve with a glass-holder.

### N° 191   SHERRY SANGAREE (HOT)
#### C GLASS

Heat up water and Sandeman sherry [60 ml each], sprinkle of nutmeg, pour into the glass and serve with a glass-holder.

### N° 192   TOM AND JERRY
#### CUP

Boil some water. In a Tom & Jerry cup, brisk a fresh egg yolk with 1 spoon [1 barspoon] of powdered sugar, fill up [160 ml] of the cup with boiling water, finish with rum and cognac Curlier in equal quantity [30 ml each] and mix by transferring back and forth from the cup to one hot vessel, not to cool the mixture and serve with all the froth by sprinkling some nutmeg.

One of America's winter classics as created by the Professor Jerry
Thomas and named after his two pet mice. Jerry used whisked egg white
in his original which does bring more texture to the drink.

### N° 193   WHISKEY PUNCH CHAUD
#### RED E GLASS
Heat up half whisky (Scotch or Irish) and water [50 ml each], 1 spoon [1 barspoon] of powdered sugar, pour into the glass and serve as it flame.

### N° 194   WHISKEY FLIP (HOT)
#### C GLASS
Brisk a fresh egg yolk with a spoon [1 barspoon] of powdered sugar, finish with Scotch whisky and water [50 ml each], heat up, pour into the glass, sprinkle some nutmeg and serve.

### N° 195   WHISKEY SLING (HOT)
#### C GLASS
Heat up in equal quantity Irish or Scotch whisky with some water [50 ml each], 1 spoon [1 barspoon] of powdered sugar, pour into the glass, sprinkle some nutmeg, cut and squeeze 2 lemon zest and serve.

### N° 196   WHISKEY TODDY
#### C GLASS
Heat up gin, water [50 ml each], 1 spoon [1 barspoon] of powdered sugar and serve without lemon in a glass-holder.

SIXTH PART

# SOCIAL GATHERING PUNCHES

AND

HOW TO PREPARE THEM

SIXTH PART

# SOCIAL GATHERING PUNCHES

I believe I shouldn't finish my American drinks manual, without forgetting some hot and cold punches recipes for social gathering, with the quantities for an establish number of people, which will be easy to increase or decrease, depending of the guest number.

For hot punches, it will be preferable to prepare them in thick clay bowls and to absolutely use them for that purpose.

For cold punches, huge bowls will do to make any drink.

Always make sure to place an abundance of fresh fruits to serve the cold punches, as well as a side display of straws.

Unlike the other drinks listed in *Bariana*, the social gathering punches are all titled in French, and I prefer to leave them that way. This is just how Louis wanted them to be. However, it does not mean all these drinks originated in France.

The collection below is a melting pot of French serves: *Punch de Tous Les Jours, Punch Nec Plus Ultra* (Latin for 'nothing more beyond'; the French later shortened it to *ne plus ultra*); Louis' own *Louis' Punch Chaud, Punch du Criterion*, a French twist on Imperial Punch called *Punch Royal*. But there are also some classic British-American recipes like *Punch a L'ananas, a l'Orange, de la Montagne*.

In many of these recipes, Louis did not specify a mixing container of any sort. I think it is safe to assume he expected us to use a punch bowl for most or all of these recipes.

To be honest with you, I did not try mixing up these grand bowls, not because this is the last chapter and I was getting tired or lazy, but purely because if you want the right sensation of these drinks you have to make them accurately--for the right number of people suggested. Cutting down everything for a sample would not be an accurate translation of the drink.

And, unfortunately, I did not have that many people around me when I practised the *Bariana* recipes. Oh well. For my next translation I'll be more organised and throw enough parties to see how the guests appreciate each one: not the free booze but the social gatherings.

## BOWL & SPOON HOLDER FOR SOCIAL PUNCHES SERVICE

Spoon Holder...... piece 45fr.
Lemon & Orange bowl
Silver plated................ Piece 40fr.

# BOL & PORTE-CUILLÈRES

pour le

## SERVICE DES PUNCHS POUR SOCIÉTÉS

**Porte-Cuillères**...... Pièce **45** fr.

**Bol à Citrons ou Oranges**
Argenté................ Pièce **40** fr.

9.

### N° 197    PUNCH SANDEMAN AU XÉRÈS
#### FOR 2 PEOPLE

Half a bottle of Sandeman sherry, 2 mouth spoons [4 barspoons] of powdered sugar, 1 thinly sliced orange, 3 lemon slices, ice well and mix, garnish with seasonal fruits, served in B glasses with straws.

### N° 198    PUNCH DE TOUS LES JOURS
#### [Everyday Punch]
#### FOR 2 PEOPLE

Crushed ice, 1 Madeira glass [60 ml] of Curlier cognac, Madeira glass [30 ml] of Bordeaux red wine, 1 liqueur glass [30 ml] of white absinthe, 1 mouth spoon [2 barspoons] of powdered sugar, 2 dashes of gomme syrup, finish with fresh water, mix well and serve in C glasses.

### N° 199    PUNCH AU CIDRE
#### FOR 10 PEOPLE

Pour a litre of Sandeman medium sherry on a dozen lemon zests, add 125 grams of powdered sugar, sprinkle in some nutmeg, add 1 bottle of cider, mix well, place the bowl on ice and when you serve it add a glass of Curlier fine champagne cognac and a few strips of cucumber rind, and serve in C glasses.

### N° 200    PUNCH IMPERIAL FRANÇAIS
#### FOR 10 PEOPLE

1 bottle of red wine, 1 bottle of soda water, 4 mouth spoons of powdered sugar, coffee spoon [barspoon] of powdered nutmeg, ice cubes, 3 pieces of cucumber rind, mix well and serve in C glasses.

### N° 201    PUNCH DE L'INDÉPENDANCE
#### FOR 12 PEOPLE

1 bottle of rye whiskey, litre of Jamaican rum, 1 litre of water, thinly slice 6 lemons, slice 1 pineapple into wedges, add sugar to taste, ice up and serve in C glasses.

## N°202   PUNCH ROYAL
### FOR 15 PEOPLE

In a huge bowl, squeeze the juice of 5 lemons and 2 medium sweet oranges, dissolve 250 grams of powdered sugar, then add the thinly peeled rind of an orange, pour slowly 6 stiff whisked egg whites, pour in a bottle of Henriot dry champagne, a bottle of Jamaican rum, mix well, garnish with seasonal fruits, put the bowl in an ice room and serve an hour later.

If you do not have an ice room, a refrigerator will work just as well.

## N°203   PUNCH AU CHAMPAGNE
### FOR 15 PEOPLE

1 bottle of red Bordeaux wine, 250 grams powdered sugar, 1 sliced up orange, the juice of a lemon [120 ml], 4 pineapple slice, 1 liqueur glass [30 ml] of raspberry syrup, mix well, seasonal fruits, pour 2 bottles of Henriot Silver label champagne and serve in champagne glasses C.

## N°204   PUNCH DU CRITERION
### FOR 15 PEOPLE

250 grams powdered sugar, 1 bottle of Curlier fine champagne cognac, 1 bottle of rum, 1 bottle of water, a litre of curaçao, juice of 4 lemons [120 ml], mix up with a huge ice block, add seasonal fruits and serve in champagne glasses C.

## N°205   PUNCH DE L'EUROPE
### FOR 15 PEOPLE

A litre of raspberry syrup, 125 grams of powdered sugar, 1 litre of water, 1.5 litres of Curlier cognac, 1 thinly sliced lemon, 1 orange sliced, 6 pineapple slices, fill up with crushed ice, garnish with fruits, orange etc., serve in C glasses with straws.

### N° 206   PUNCH DE FEU M. TOUPINEL
#### FOR 20 PEOPLE

6 thinly sliced lemons, 2 bottles of rum, 2 bottles of Curlier cognac, 500 grams of powdered sugar, 2.5 litres of water, and a litre of boiled milk.

Macerate the lemons with the cognac and rum for twenty-four hours, then add the sugar, water and the milk till mixed, and then clarified.

This punch can be bottled and used hot or cold.

> Louis may have meant "add water and milk until mixed, then clarify it" but it is hard to tell.

### N° 207   PUNCH A L'ANANAS
#### FOR 20 PEOPLE

4 bottles of Henriot dry champagne, litre Curlier fine champagne cognac, 1 litre Jamaican rum, 1 Madeira glass [60 ml] of curaçao, juice of 4 lemons [120 ml], 4 sliced up pineapples, powdered sugar to taste.

Put the pineapple slices in a huge bowl, sprinkle with sugar, and when the sugar as completely dissolved in the pineapple, add the rest of the ingredients except the champagne and leave it in an ice room [fridge] for about an hour, then add the champagne with a huge ice block placed in the middle and garnish with seasonal fruits and sliced oranges, serve in C glasses.

### N° 208   PUNCH A L'ORANGE
#### FOR 20 PEOPLE

Squeeze 4 oranges [240 ml], the rind of 1 orange, 500 grams of sugar cubes, 1 litre of boiling water, leave it macerate for an hour, add a litre of pale ale, a litre Curlier cognac, add a little boiling water and perfume with noyaux, put it in an ice room [fridge] then pour and serve in C glasses.

We can make a lemon punch in the same way by replacing the oranges with lemons.

### N° 209   PUNCH DE LA MONTAGNE
#### FOR 20 PEOPLE

5 bottles of Jules Mumm champagne, half a bottle of Jamaican rum, a litre of maraschino, 6 sliced up lemons, sugar to taste, mix well, place an ice block in the middle of bowl, garnish with oranges, lemons, cherries preserved in eau-de-vie, candy sugar, etc., and serve.

Here is a delicious punch to celebrate the new year!

### N° 210   PUNCH DE LA GARDE NATIONALE DE NEW-YORK
### (LE NATIONAL GUARD N.Y. PUNCH)
#### FOR 30 PEOPLE

3 bottles of Jules Mumm champagne, 1 bottle of Sandeman dry sherry, 1 bottle of Curlier fine de champagne cognac, 1 bottle of Sauternes (Château Peyron), 1 thinly sliced pineapple, 4 thinly sliced lemons, sugar to taste, mix well with a huge ice block and serve immediately.

### N° 211   PUNCH DE COLOMBIE
#### FOR 30 PEOPLE

3 bottles of Henriot dry champagne, 1 bottle of curaçao, 1 bottle of Curlier cognac, 1 bottle of Jamaican rum, 2 bottles of Sandeman Madeira, 2 bottles of soda water, 1 kilo of raisins, add some orange and lemon slices, candy sugar, a little strong-brewed green tea, leave in an ice room [fridge] for 2 hours, mix well, ice and serve in B glasses.

### N°212   PUNCH NEC PLUS ULTRA
#### FOR 60 PEOPLE

6 bottles of red Bordeaux wine, 6 bottles of soda water, 1 bottle of Curlier fine champagne cognac, 1 bottle of Sandeman sherry, a litre of strong-brewed green tea, juice of 3 lemons [90 ml], half a pineapple cut in small pieces, sugar to taste, mix well, let it set, strain and bottle, keep for a month before serving.

### N°213   PUNCH EUGÈNE BARDIOT ESQ.
#### FOR 80 PEOPLE

1 kilo of powdered sugar, 6 bottles of soda water, 6 bottles of Henriot champagne, 2 bottles of Bordeaux red wine, 4 bottles of Rhine wine, 1 bottle of Curlier cognac, 4 bottles of filtered water, 3 thinly sliced lemons, 1 pineapple, 4 oranges, mix well, add ice cubes and serve in B glasses with seasonal fruits and straws.

### N°214   LOUIS' PUNCH CHAUD
#### FOR 12 PEOPLE

A litre of strong-brewed green tea, litre of Curlier cognac, 1 liqueur glass of curaçao, juice of 2 lemons [60 ml], sugar to taste, 125 grams of calfs foot jelly, heat up and serve in C glasses.

Drink as hot as possible.

### N°215   PUNCH CHAUD AU COGNAC
#### FOR 15 PEOPLE

A litre of Jamaican rum, a litre of Curlier cognac, 500 grams of sugar cubes, 4 lemons sliced, 1 litre of water, 1 coffee spoon of powdered nutmeg, heat well, stirring intermittently, and serve in C glasses with glass holder.

# FINAL NOTE

I hope you enjoyed the piece and the work done to it, I never wrote a book before and this is my first translation ever. I'm not sure what's harder, trying to put yourself into somebody else's work done 100 years ago, transmitting his voice and craft or writing freely what's in your mind. ...

Well, I'll tell you when I'll do my own book, one day.

—Charles Vexenat

**Coupe à Sucre** (haute)

| MÉTAL BLANC | | Avivé | | Argenté | |
|---|---|---|---|---|---|
| Diamètre 0ᵐ07 Pièce | | 4 | » | 7 | » |
| » 0ᵐ09 » | | 6 | » | 9 | » |
| » 0ᵐ10 » | | 8 | » | 11 | » |

**Coupe à Sucre** (creuse)

| MÉTAL BLANC | | Avivé | | Argenté |
|---|---|---|---|---|
| Diamètre 0ᵐ07 Pièce | | 3 | » | 4.50 |
| » 0ᵐ08 » | | 4 | » | 5.50 |
| » 0ᵐ09 » | | 5 | » | 6.50 |

**Coupe à Sandwichs**..... **02 fr.**
Cloche   »    ..... **26 fr.**

**Coupe à Sucre** (basse)

| MÉTAL BLANC | | Avivé | Argenté | |
|---|---|---|---|---|
| Diamètre 0ᵐ07 Pièce | | 2.25 | 3 | » |
| » 0ᵐ08 » | | 2.75 | 3.50 | |
| » 0ᵐ09 » | | 3 | 4 | » |

**Sucrier**, forme Coupe

Petit modèle...... Pièce **23 fr.**
Moyen   «   ...... » **29** »
Grand   »   ...... » **32** »

**Lampe à Cigares**
Pièce.................. **26 fr.**

**Porte Cure-dents**
Pièce................ **5 fr. 50**

**Fontaine à Thé et á Café**
Pièce................ 375 fr.

**Pince à Sucre**
Modèle uni, pince légère
Avivé   2 fr. 25 | Argenté   5 fr.

**Etiquette**
Avec inscription gravée
Pièce...   4 fr.

**Grande Carafe**
Cristal taillé (pour liqueur)
Pièce.....   12 fr.

**Fouchon à vis**
pour  grande  Carafe
Pièce...   4 fr.

**Godet à Absinthe**
Métal blanc avivé Pièce   4 fr. 50
»       »  argenté  »      6 fr.

**Fontaine à Thé et à Café**

Pièce................. **375** fr.

**Pince à Sucre**

Modèle uni, pince légère

Avivé  **2** fr. **25** | Argenté  **5** fr.

**Etiquette**

Avec inscription gravée

Pièce...  **4** fr.

**Grande Carafe**

Cristal taillé (pour liqueur)

Pièce.....  **12** fr.

**Bouchon à vis**

pour grande Carafe

Pièce...  **4** fr.

**Godet à Absinthe**

Métal blanc avivé Pièce  **4** fr. **50**

»  » argenté »  **6** fr.

**Grand Pitcher à Bascule**
Avec doublure étanche... Pièce **350** fr.

**1/2 Pinte à Bière**
Pièce **23** fr.
**Pinte** .... Pièce **30** fr.

**1/2 Pinte** unie
Pièce **18** fr.
**Pinte** unie Pièce **26** fr.

**Porte Soda-Water**
Métal blanc avivé. Pièce **8** fr.
      »       argenté   »   **11** fr.

| MÉTAL BLANC | Avivé | Argenté |
|---|---|---|
| Contenance 8 tasses Pièce | **29** » | **47** » |
| »   12   »   » | **35** » | **58** » |

**Service à Thé** (Five o'clock tea)

Composition, pour 2 à 6 personnes
Théière, Sucrier, Pot à lait, Bouilloire, Pince à sucre
Le tout sur 1 plateau argenté.

| | | |
|---|---|---|
| Service 2 pers. | **230** fr. |
| » 4 » | **240** » |
| » 6 » | **260** » |

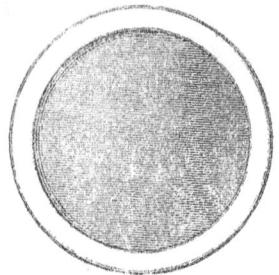

**Plateaux carres** (pour Services)

| MÉTAL BLANC | | Avivé | Argenté |
|---|---|---|---|
| Longueur 0m30 | pièce | 9.50 | 33 » |
| » 0m40 | » | 16 » | 50 » |
| » 0m45 | » | 23 » | 65 » |

**Plateaux ronds** (pour Services)

| MÉTAL BLANC | | Avivé | Argenté |
|---|---|---|---|
| Diamètre 25c pièce | | 6 » | 18 |
| » 30c » | | 8 » | 26 |
| » 35c » | | 10 » | 36 |

Avivé..... **6** fr.
Argenté... **9** fr.

# USTENSILES POUR LE CHAMPAGNE

**Seau à Champagne**
Pour bouteille.. pièce **47** »
» ½ » .. » **42** »

**Bouchon automatique**
pour Champagne et Boissons gazeuses
Breveté s g. d. g.

Bouchon uni pièce **5.50**
» av. crochets » **6.75**
» et tire-bouch. » **7.25**

**Support pour Champagne**
Support nickelé ... .. pièce **38** »
» argenté.. ... » **44** »

**Poinçon pour Champagne**
Pièce . ................ **2** fr. **25**

# THE ORIGINAL FRENCH TEXT

# INTRODUCTION

———○———

Il n'y a pas de pays dans le Monde entier où il existe autant de variétés dans les boissons qu'en Amérique. Leurs préparations si peu connues de nous et si souvent mal employées par des Barmen se disant compétents dans ces mélanges, faisaient délaisser complètement par nos amateurs toutes ces mixtures délicieuses pour d'autres apéritifs si souvent nuisibles à la santé.

Je suis heureux aujourd'hui de pouvoir fournir à mes lecteurs, après quelques années d'expériences, un recueil complet leur permettant de faire à première vue les boissons les plus difficiles et absolument dans les mêmes conditions que les plus célèbres Barmen de l'Amérique.

C'est ainsi que le limonadier pourra faire selon le désir du client n'importe quelles boissons, que le maître d'hôtel préparera un bon Cocktail avant un délicieux dîner et que les maîtresses de maison toujours embarrassées pourront offrir, aux amies qui leur rendent visite, quelques boissons rafraîchissantes et sans danger.

Les hommes trouveront par leur usage le stimulant nécessaire, les dames les fraîcheurs délicieuses de la santé et les enfants la saveur et les douceurs dont ils sont si friands.

J'ai divisé mon livre en six parties bien distinctes :

1° **Les Cocktails**, boissons apéritives ;

2° **Les Short Drinks**, boissons que l'on prépare dans des verres de moyenne grandeur en général et que l'on peut prendre à toute heure de la journée comme consommations de fantaisie ;

3° **Les Cobblers et les Punchs**, boissons glacées généralement ornées de fruits, recommandées pendant les fortes chaleurs ;

4° **Les Summer Drinks**, boissons d'été que l'on ne peut employer que durant la saison des fruits ;

5° **Les Winter Drinks**, boissons d'hiver, chaudes et réconfortantes ;

6° **Les Punchs** pour sociétés avec les quantités nécessaires pour un nombre déterminé de personnes.

Afin de faciliter leur usage, chaque recette portera d'abord un numéro d'ordre se rapportant à la table des matières et une lettre se rapportant au tableau des verres ci-après, que l'on n'aura qu'à consulter afin d'employer un verre de la contenance nécessaire et les récipients dans lesquels on doit mélanger.

Tous les modèles d'ustensiles de Bar, ainsi que la verrerie, se trouvent intercalés dans ce livre et je me mets à la disposition des personnes désireuses d'en obtenir dans le plus bref délai, grâce à un stock que j'ai cru devoir faire venir d'Amérique pour satisfaire mes lecteurs et lectrices.

Louis FOUQUET

# VERRES A EMPLOYER ET LEUR CONTENANCE

**A**

**Verre à mélange**
Contenance Eau : 500 grammes.

**B**

**Verre à Cobbler, rouge et blanc**
Contenance Eau : 250 gr.

**C**

**Gobelet blanc, rouge et vert**
Contenance Eau : 125 gr.

**D**

**Verre à Cocktail**
Contenance Eau : 90 grammes.

**E**

**Verre blanc, rouge et vert**
Contenance Eau : 100 grammes.

**F**

**Verre rouge**
Contenance Eau : 60 gr.

**G**

**Verre flûte** Contenance Eau : 30 gr.

**Chaque Recette indique par une lettre le Verre qu'il faut employer**

# PREMIÈRE PARTIE

# LES COCKTAILS

et leurs

# PRÉPARATIONS

# PREMIÈRE PARTIE

## LE COCKTAIL

Le Cocktail, ce précieux breuvage si goûté de tous nos fins gourmets, est un des meilleurs apéritifs lorsqu'il est fait suivant les règles de l'art.

Le "Cock-a-tailer" comme les Italiens appellent un Cocktail, est une boisson essentiellement américaine et son mélange est la première leçon à donner à un jeune Barman avant de passer aux autres breuvages si variés et qui ne demandent pas tant de soins et de raffinements.

Pour faire un bon Cocktail il faut surtout avoir une table garnie des objets suivants :

1° Quelques flacons à essences avec bouchons stilligoutte (voir figure 3), afin de verser par traits et qui contiendront : **absinthe Cusenier** — **curaçao Cusenier** — **crème de noyau Cusenier** — **angostura** — **orange bitter** et **extrait de quinquina**, etc.;

2° Un verre à mélange (voir verre A) assez fort du bas pour résister aux chocs de la cuillère avec laquelle vous battez le liquide ;

3° Une cuillère (figure 2, page 15) arrondie du bas, facilitant les mélanges ;

4° Une passoire (figure 4, page 15) pour séparer la glace des boissons avant de servir ;

5° Un gobelet argent à Cocktail (figure 5, page 15), avec couvercle à passoire pour les personnes désireuses du Cocktail frappé.

Enfin, pour faire un bon Cocktail, voici comment il faut procéder :

Prenez votre verre à mélange, mettez quelques petits morceaux de glace, prenez vos flacons stilligoutte par le goulot, entre l'index et le majeur et versez par trait vos essences indiquées, puis le liquide auquel vous désirez que votre Cocktail soit : cognac ou whisky ou gin, etc.

Agiter ensuite avec votre cuillère à cocktail, adapter la passoire et verser dans un verre, en ayant soin de ne pas laisser passer le moindre morceau de glace. Si le coup d'œil est bon, vous devez remplir votre verre exactement, sans en laisser une goutte dans votre verre à mélange.

Si vous n'avez pas confiance en vous, faites votre cocktail dans le verre qui doit être servi, en ayant soin de le vider ensuite dans votre verre à mélange pour le glacer convenablement et le repasser de nouveau dans votre premier verre, de la sorte vous arriverez très juste en n'ayant aucune perte ; c'est la manière la plus employée par les personnes qui ne pratiquent guère. De la façon première, en certains moments de presse, vous avez économie de temps, mais il faut avoir la dextérité qui ne s'obtient qu'en pratiquant beaucoup.

Lorsque votre cocktail est servi, vous coupez délicatement et en fine lame un zeste de citron que vous cassez légèrement en deux dans la longueur au-dessus du liquide, afin d'en faire jaillir le jus et que vous laissez tomber ensuite dans le fond du verre. De la sorte votre cocktail a un léger parfum de citron qui est toujours très apprécié. J'ai souvent vu des Barmen qui pressaient un zeste de citron en dehors du verre et qui le mettaient ensuite dans le cocktail, croyant alors que ce n'était absolument que pour l'œil et que le cocktail n'avait nullement besoin de ce dernier raffinement. C'est un bien grand tort.

Lorsque vous servez un Cocktail à une dame, il est toujours préférable d'avoir soin de sucrer les parois du verre, en passant légèrement les bords sur une tranche de citron fraîchement coupée et en trempant délicatement ensuite dans le sucre en poudre, ce qui donne une apparence de givre collé qui flatte si gentiment les lèvres et les yeux.

Pour les Cocktails frappés, il suffit d'employer le gobelet (figure 5) au lieu du verre à mélange et d'agiter fortement des deux mains de bas en haut, vous avez alors un Cocktail fortement glacé, mais qui n'est pas si agréable au goût que par la manière précédente.

# USTENSILES POUR COCKTAILS

Figure 2
### Cuillère à Cocktail
Pièce... **5** fr.

**Bouchon**
Pièce.. **3** fr.

Figure 3

**Bouteille à Bitter** Angostura
Avec bouchon stilligoutte
Pièce...... **7** fr. **50**

Figure 4

**Cuillère passoire**
Pièce... **9** fr.

Figure 5

### Gobelet à Cocktail
Avec Couvercle à passoire

Pièce................... **26** francs

Pour servir un Cocktail

**N° 1**

## ALABAZAM COCKTAIL
### Verre D

Prendre le verre à mélange A, glace en petits morceaux, 4 traits d'angostura, 8 traits de curaçao, 4 gouttes de jus de citron. Remplir avec cognac Curlier, bien agiter avec cuillère, passer, verser zeste de citron et servir.

**N° 2**

## ABSINTHE COCKTAIL
### Verre C

Prendre le verre à mélange A, glace en petits morceaux, 4 traits d'angostura, 2 traits de curaçao Cusenier, une cuillerée à café d'anisette, absinthe blanche Cusenier et eau en égale quantité, bien agiter, passer, verser zeste de citron et servir.

N. B. — Il est préférable d'employer l'absinthe blanche à la verte en raison de la couleur que donne le mélange, le goût en est absolument le même; la blanche donne une couleur rosée superbe et la verte une couleur grisâtre et peu appétissante.

**N° 3**

## ANGLER'S COCKTAIL
### Verre D

Prendre le verre à mélange A, glace en petits morceaux, 3 traits d'angostura, 6 traits d'orange (bitter), une cuillerée à café de sirop de framboises, finir avec du gin, agiter, passer, verser, zeste de citron et servir.

**N° 4**

## APPETIZER COCKTAIL
### Verre D

Prendre le verre à mélange A, glace en petits morceaux,

4 traits d'angostura, une cuillerée à café de sucre en poudre, 2 traits de jus de citron, finir avec du scotch whisky, agiter, passer, verser, zeste de citron et servir.

**N° 5**       **BRANDY COCKTAIL**

VERRE D

Prendre le verre à mélange A, glace en petits morceaux. 2 traits d'angostura, 3 traits de crème de noyau, 3 traits de curaçao Cusenier, finir avec fine champagne Curlier, agiter, passer, verser, zeste de citron et servir.

**N° 6**       **BOURBON WHISKY COCKTAIL**

VERRE D

Prendre le verre à mélange A, glace en petits morceaux, 2 traits d'angostura, 4 traits crème de noyaux Cusenier, 3 traits de curaçao, finir avec du Bourbon Whisky, agiter, passer, verser, zeste de citron et servir.

**N° 7**       **BOMBAY COCKTAIL**

VERRE D

Prendre le verre à mélange A, glace en petits morceaux, 3 traits d'angostura, 3 traits crème de noyaux, 4 traits de curaçao, une cuillerée à café de sucre poudre, finir avec du cognac Curlier, bien agiter, passer, verser, zeste de citron et servir.

**N° 8**       **CHAMPAGNE COCKTAIL**

VERRE C

Prendre le verre C, mettre un petit morceau de glace, 3 traits de curaçao, 2 traits d'angostura, zeste de citron. Remplir avec du champagne Henriot, Sillery sec, agiter légèrement, chalumeaux et servir.

# FINE CHAMPAGNE

| GRAND PRIX | | ANVERS 1894 |
|---|---|---|
| EXPOSITION UNIVERSELLE | **COGNAC** | PARIS & ALGER |
| MÉDAILLE D'OR | | 1889 |

# COURVOISIER & CURLIER Frères

## MAISONS :

| PARIS | LONDRES |
|---|---|
| 58, Quai de Bercy, 58 | St-Dunstan's Buildings |
| | E. C. |

## JARNAC (Charente)

Agences dans toutes les grandes villes du Monde

**N° 9**        ## COFFEE COCKTAIL
### Verre C

Prendre le verre à mélange A, glace en petits morceaux, 3 traits de sirop de gomme, 4 traits de noyaux. une cuillerée à bouche de fine champagne Curlier, finir avec café, bien agiter, passer, verser, saupoudrer de muscade et servir dans verre C.

**N° 10**       ## CHINESE COCKTAIL
### Verre D

Prendre le verre à mélange A, glace en petits morceaux, 2 traits d'angostura, 4 traits de noyaux, 4 traits de curaçao, une cuillerée à café de sucre en poudre, finir avec cognac Curlier et rhum en égale quantité, bien agiter, passer, verser, zeste de citron et servir.

**N° 11**       ## EAST INDIA COCKTAIL
### Verre D

Prendre le verre à mélange A, glace en petits morceaux, une cuillerée à café de curaçao, de sirop d'ananas et de marasquin, 3 traits d'angostura, finir avec cognac Curlier, agiter, passer, verser, zeste de citron et servir.

**N° 12**       ## GIN COCKTAIL
### Verre D

Prendre le verre à mélange A, glace en petits morceaux, 3 traits d'angostura bitter, 3 traits de curaçao, 3 traits de crème de noyaux, finir avec du gin vieux, agiter, passer, verser, zeste de citron et servir.

N° 13    IRISH WHISKY COCKTAIL
Verre D

Prendre le verre à mélange A, glace en petits morceaux, 2 traits d'angostura, 3 traits de crème de noyaux, 3 traits de curaçao, finir avec le gin, agiter, passer, verser, zeste de citron et servir.

N° 14    JAPANESE COCKTAIL
Verre D

Prendre le verre à mélange A, glace en petits morceaux, 2 traits d'angostura, 3 traits de crème de noyaux, 3 traits de curaçao, une petite cuillerée de sirop d'orgeat, finir avec du cognac Curlier, agiter, passer, verser, zeste de citron et servir.

N° 15    JERSEY COCKTAIL
Verre C

Prendre le verre à mélange A, glace en petits morceaux, une petite cuillerée de sucre en poudre, 3 traits d'angostura, 1 trait de curaçao, 1 trait de crème de noyaux, une petite cuillerée de cognac Curlier, finir avec du cidre, bien agiter, passer, verser, zeste de citron et servir.

N° 16    LADIE'S COCKTAIL
Verre rouge D

Prendre le verre à mélange A, glace en petits morceaux, une petite cuillerée de sucre en poudre et d'anisette, 3 traits de menthe verte, 3 traits de curaçao, finir avec kirsch et eau en égale quantité, agiter, passer, verser, demi-tranche d'orange et servir.

**MÉDAILLE D'OR**

*Exposition Internationale d'Hygiène, Vienne (Autriche) 1894*

**DIPLOME D'HONNEUR**

*Exposition Internationale, Amsterdam 1895*

**DIPLOME D'HONNEUR**

*Exposition Internationale, Innsbruck (Autriche) 1896*

### N° 17     LOUIS' QUINA COCKTAIL
#### Verre D

Prendre le verre à mélange A, glace en petits morceaux, 6 traits d'extrait de quinquina, 2 traits de curaçao, finir avec quinquina Dubonnet, agiter, passer, verser et servir sans mettre de zeste de citron.

### N° 18     MARTINI COCKTAIL
#### Verre D

Le plus apprécié des Cocktails lorsque l'on observe bien les quantités suivantes :

Prendre le verre à mélange A, glace en petits morceaux, 4 traits d'orange bitter, 2 traits d'absinthe, 3 traits de curaçao, 3 traits de crème de noyaux, finir avec gin et vermouth de Turin en égale quantité, agiter, passer, verser, zeste de citron et servir.

### N° 19     MANHATTAN COCKTAIL
#### Verre D

Prendre le verre à mélange A, glace en petits morceaux, 2 traits d'angostura, 2 traits de noyaux, 3 traits de curaçao, finir avec rye whisky et vermouth de Turin en quantité égale, agiter, passer, verser, zeste de citron et servir.

### N° 20     MARTINICAN VERMOUTH COCKTAIL
#### Verre D

Prendre le verre à mélange A, glace en petits morceaux, 2 traits d'angostura, 2 traits de curaçao, 2 traits de noyaux, une petite cuillerée de sirop d'ananas, finir avec vermouth de Turin et rhum en égale quantité, agiter, passer, verser, zeste de citron et servir.

### N° 21    MORNING GLORY COCKTAIL
#### Verre C

Prendre le verre à mélange A, glace en petits morceaux, 2 traits d'angostura, 3 traits de noyaux, 3 traits de curaçao, 1 trait d'absinthe Cusenier, une petite cuillerée de sucre, puis verser scotch whisky et cognac Curlier en égale quantité, agiter, passer, verser, zeste de citron, finir avec de l'eau de seltz et servir.

### N° 22    NAPOLÉON'S OWN COCKTAIL
#### Verre C

Prendre grand verre à mélange A, glace en petits morceaux, une petite cuillerée de sirop de sucre, une de jus de citron, whisky et gin en égale quantité, agiter, passer, verser, zeste de citron. Remplir avec du siphon et servir.

### N° 23    RYE WHISKY COCKTAIL
#### Verre D

Prendre grand verre à mélange A, glace en petits morceaux, 3 traits de curaçao, 3 traits de noyaux, 2 traits d'angostura, finir avec du rye whisky, agiter, passer, verser, zeste de citron et servir.

### N° 24    SHERRY COCKTAIL
#### (Cocktail au vin de Xérès)
#### Verre D

Prendre grand verre à mélange A, glace en petits morceaux, 3 traits de curaçao, 3 de noyaux, 2 traits d'angostura, finir avec du sherry Sandeman, agiter, passer, verser, zeste de citron et servir.

# Installations de Bars, Brasseries, Hôtels

Nº 25 ## LOUIS SPECIAL COCKTAIL
### Verre D

Dans un verre à mélange A, glace en petits morceaux, 3 traits de curaçao, de noyaux et d'angostura, verser moitié gin, moitié vermouth de Turin, presser une demi-orange, bien agiter, passer, verser, zeste de citron et servir.

Nº 26 ## SODA COCKTAIL
### Verre B

Le Soda Cocktail est surtout recommandé pour les estomacs délicats. Avant un repas, il donnera l'appétit si l'on a déjà l'estomac chargé par différents apéritifs; après, il facilitera la digestion et, pris d'un trait, donnera une douce fraîcheur dans tout le corps et rétablira l'ordre des fonctions nutritives et digestives.

Prendre un verre à Cobbler (verre B), y mettre un morceau de glace, 6 traits d'angostura, 4 de curaçao et 2 de noyaux, presser un zeste de citron et verser un Soda qui n'aura nullement perdu son gaz; au moment de boire, remuer avec une cuillerée à café de sucre en poudre et boire d'un trait au moment de l'effervescence.

Nº 27 ## SARATOGA COCKTAIL
### Verre D

Prendre grand verre à mélange A, glace en petits morceaux, 2 traits d'angostura, de curaçao et de noyaux, finir avec cognac Curlier, scoth whisky et vermouth en quantité égale, bien agiter, passer, verser, demi-tranche de citron et servir.

N° 28       **VERMOUTH COCKTAIL**

Verre D

Prendre grand verre à mélange A, glace en petits morceuux, 2 traits d'angostura, 3 de noyaux et 4 de curaçao, finir avec vermouth de Turin, bien agiter, passer, verser, zeste de citron et servir.

N° 29       **VICTORIA COCKTAIL**

Verre D

Prendre grand verre à mélange A, glace en petits morceaux, une petite cuillerée de sucre poudre, 6 traits de menthe verte, finir avec cognac Curlier et rhum en quantité égale, bien agiter, passer, verser, ajouter une petite branche de menthe poivré ou une tranche d'orange, suivant la saison, et servir.

N° 30       **WHISKY COCKTAIL**

Verre D

Prendre grand verre à mélange A, glace en petits morceaux, 3 traits d'angostura, de noyaux et de curaçao, finir avec scotch whisky, bien agiter, passer, verser, zeste de citron et servir.

# DEUXIÈME PARTIE

# SHORT DRINKS

### et leurs

# PRÉPARATIONS

# DEUXIÈME PARTIE

———

# SHORT DRINKS

———

Sont ainsi nommées toutes les boissons de fantaisie, servies à toute heure de la journée, que l'on peut prendre sans aucune crainte aussi bien avant qu'après les repas; généralement servies dans des verres de moyenne grandeur (verres E. C. F. G.), elles sont remarquables par leur composition. Un grand nombre sont faites avec des jaunes ou des blancs d'œufs; celles-ci sont donc excellentes pour l'estomac et souvent ordonnées par des médecins compétents qui ont des clients trop gourmets pour se passer entièrement de boire entre les repas, à cause de maux d'estomacs ou autres, occasionnés souvent par l'abus de mauvais alcools ou d'amers plutôt nuisibles qu'hygiéniques.

Pour fabriquer toutes ces précieuses compositions, il est nécessaire d'ajouter à votre buffet quelques autres ustensiles indispensables pour la réussite de tous ces mélanges.

Il est donc bon de se munir :

1° D'une série de gobelets en argent s'emboîtant les uns

dans les autres et permettant de pouvoir frapper fortement, comme l'indique la figure n° 1 ;

2° Un flacon pour épices (page 35), dans lequel on mettra de la muscade en poudre, afin de pouvoir saupoudrer les boissons qui l'exigent ;

3° Un batteur pour blancs d'œufs comme il en existe un dans tous les ménages ;

4° Une série de verres E. C. F. G., de différentes couleurs que l'on devra employer lorsque la couleur grisâtre d'un mélange l'exigera.

Comme pour les Cocktails, les personnes ne pouvant faire à vue d'œil les boissons directement dans les gobelets argent, feront mieux en préparant directement dans les verres indiqués pour le service et frapper ensuite pour reverser après, en ayant toujours soin de ne pas laisser passer la glace.

# USTENSILES POUR LA COMPOSITION
# DES SHORT DRINKS

**Flacon** pour Epices          **Râpe à Muscade**

Pièce............... **6** fr.       Pièce.. ........... **15** fr.

Figure 1

**Gobelets pour Boissons** (3 grandeurs)

Le jeu.......... **70** fr.

Pour frapper une Boisson

## N° 31     BOSOM CARESSER
### Verre B

Prendre un gobelet argent, glace en petits morceaux, 1 jaune d'œuf bien frais, une cuillerée à café de grenadine et de marasquin, une cuillerée à bouche de cognac Curlier, finir avec du sherry, frapper fortement en ajustant le gobelet grandeur au-dessus, passer et servir.

## N° 32     BLACK STRIPE
### Verre rose B

Prendre gobelet argent, glace en morceaux, 2 cuillerées à café de mélasse, finir avec eau et scotch whisky, frapper fortement, passer, saupoudrer de muscade et servir.

## N° 33     BRANDY SHANTERALLA
### Verre jaune E

Prendre gobelet argent, glace en morceaux, une cuillerée à bouche de curaçao, une cuillerée à bouche de chartreuse jaune, 2 cuillerées à bouche d'anisette, une cuillerée à café de sucre poudre, finir avec cognac Curlier, bien frapper, passer et servir.

## N° 34     BOMBAY PUNCHET
### Verre jaune E

Prendre gobelet argent, glace, une cuillerée à café de sucre poudre, 4 traits de marasquin, 4 traits de jus de citron, demi-verre à liqueur de cognac Curlier, finir avec du sherry Sandeman, bien frapper, passer et servir.

N° 35      **BRANDY DAISY**

VERRE C

Prendre gobelet argent, glace, une cuillerée à café de sucre poudre, 3 traits de jus de citron, 1 jet de siphon, 1 verre à liqueur de chartreuse jaune, finir avec du cognac Curlier, bien frapper, passer et servir.


N° 36      **BOSTON FLIP**

VERRE C

Prendre gobelet argent, glace, une cuillerée de sucre en poudre, casser un œuf entier bien frais, finir avec du rye whisky, frapper fortement, passer et servir après avoir saupoudré un peu de muscade.


N° 37      **BRANDY AND HONEY**

VERRE C

Prendre un verre C, y mettre un petit morceau de glace, une cuillerée à café de miel, remplir avec du cognac Curlier, bien remuer avec une cuillère, placer une tranche de citron et servir.


N° 38      **BRANDY SCAFFA**

VERRE G

Prendre un verre flûte G, verser tout doucement moitié marasquin et cognac, 2 traits d'angostura sur la surface et servir.

**N° 39**     ### BRANDY CHAMPARELLE
#### VERRE G

Prendre un verre flûte G et verser en quantité égale : curaçao, chartreuse jaune, anisette, kirsch ou cognac Curlier.

Il est préférable de verser sur le dos d'une cuillère, afin de ne pas mélanger ces quatre liqueurs qui doivent être parfaitement distinctes les unes des autres.

**N° 40**     ### BRANDY FLIP
#### VERRE C

Prendre un gobelet argent, glace, 3 traits de curaçao, 3 traits de noyaux, une cuillerée à café de sucre en poudre, casser un œuf, y mettre le jaune, finir avec du cognac Curlier, frapper fortement, passer, verser et saupoudrer de muscade avant de servir.

**N° 41**     ### SPECIAL COFFEE COCKTAIL
#### VERRE C

Ce Cocktail est un Short Drink très apprécié des Américains comme digestif et demande à être servi extrêmement glacé.

Prendre un gobelet argent, glace, 2 traits de curaçao, 2 traits de noyaux, 1 œuf bien frais, une cuillerée à café de sucre poudre, finir avec Porto rouge Sandeman et cognac Curlier, frapper fortement, passer et servir, après avoir saupoudré de muscade.

Voici une boisson américaine assez originale puisque ni café ni bitter ne se trouve dans sa composition, mais elle doit son nom à sa couleur qui est exactement comme du café, lorsqu'elle est bien faite et comme je l'indique ci-dessus.

### Nº 42 — CORPSE REVIVER
#### Verre G

Cette consommation de fantaisie et si originale est d'autant plus difficile à faire que tous les produits, vendus dans différents endroits, ne sont jamais exactement de la densité voulue en alcool. Voici de quoi cette boisson est composée : il s'agit de verser au moyen du dos d'une petite cuillère, afin de ne rien mélanger, 13 liqueurs successivement et par leur couleur bien les distinguer les unes des autres : **grenadine, framboise, anisette, fraise, menthe blanche, chartreuse verte, cherry brandy, prunelle, kummel, guignolet, kirsch** et **cognac** Curlier.

Il est facile de placer ses liqueurs en essayant plusieurs fois ou les peser avant de les employer, afin d'arriver à un bon résultat.

### Nº 43 — COAXER
#### Verre C

Prendre un gobelet argent, glace en petits morceaux, une cuillerée à café de sucre en poudre, presser demi-citron, mettre un blanc d'œuf bien frais et finir avec du scotch whisky, bien frapper, passer, verser et servir.

### Nº 44 — CHAMPAGNE SOUR
#### Verre C

Prendre gobelet argent, glace en petits morceaux, une cuillerée à café de sucre poudre, 2 traits de jus de citron, puis un peu d'eau, bien frapper, passer, verser. Remplir le verre avec du champagne en y ajoutant une tranche d'orange et d'ananas et quelques fruits, durant la saison, chalumeaux et servir.

# BOUCHARD AINÉ & FILS

## Propriétaires de Vignobles

## à *BEAUNE (Côte-d'Or)*

~~~

# Grands Vins
### de
# Bourgogne

## MAISON FONDÉE EN 1750

## SUCCURSALE HALLE AUX VINS

## 27, Rue de la Côte-d'Or, 27

## PARIS

Nᵒ 45                 **COLUMBIA SKIN**

Verre rouge E

Prendre gobelet argent, glace, une cuillerée à café de sucre poudre, 2 traits de jus de citron, un peu d'eau, finir avec du rhum, bien frapper, passer, verser, une tranche de citron et servir.

Nᵒ 46                     **EGG SOUR**

Verre C

Prendre gobelet argent, glace en petits morceaux, 4 traits d'angostura, une petite cuillerée de sucre poudre, 1 œuf entier bien frais, 1 petit verre à liqueur de cognac Curlier, une cuillerée à café de sirop de gomme, finir avec du jus de citron, bien frapper, passer, verser et servir.

Nᵒ 47                     **EGG FLIP**

Verre C

Prendre gobelet argent, glace en petits morceaux, 1 jaune d'œuf bien frais, 2 traits de curaçao, 2 traits de noyaux, 2 cuillerées à café de sucre poudre, finir avec cognac Curlier et sherry Sandeman en quantité égale, bien frapper, passer, verser, saupoudrer de muscade et servir.

Nᵒ 48                   **EYE OPENER**

Verre C

Prendre gobelet argent, glace en petits morceaux, une cuillerée de sucre en poudre, un œuf bien frais, finir avec cognac Curlier et rhum, bien frapper, passer, verser, saupoudrer de muscade et servir.

## N° 49     FOUQUET'S POUSSE-CAFÉ
### Verre G

Prendre un verre G, verser doucement au moyen du dos d'une cuillère : kirsch, curaçao et fine champagne Curlier.

## N° 50     GIN SOUR
### Verre C

Prendre gobelet argent, glace en petits morceaux, une cuillerée de sucre poudre, 2 cuillerées à bouche de jus de citron, finir avec moitié gin, moitié eau, bien frapper, passer, demi-tranche de citron et servir.

## N° 51     GOLDEN FIZZ
### Verre C

Prendre gobelet argent, glace en petits morceaux, 1 jaune d'œuf bien frais, 2 cuillerées à café de sucre poudre, finir avec vieux gin et eau de seltz, bien frapper, passer, verser, demi-tranche de citron et servir.

## N° 52     GIN AND MOLASSES
### Verre C

Prendre un verre C, y mettre une cuillerée à café de gomme, une cuillerée de mélasse, verser le gin sans emplir le verre, afin de pouvoir mettre de l'eau au gré du client et servir.

## N° 53     GIN FIZZ
### Verre C

Prendre gobelet argent, glace en petits morceaux, une cuillerée à bouche de jus de citron, un verre à liqueur de gin, bien frapper, passer, verser. Remplir le verre avec de l'eau de seltz, demi-tranche de citron et servir.

## N° 54        GIN FLIP
### Verre C

Prendre un gobelet argent, glace en petits morceaux, 2 cuillerées à café de sucre en poudre, 1 jaune d'œuf bien frais, 2 traits de crème de noyaux, finir avec du old tom gin, bien frapper, passer, verser, servir en ayant saupoudré de muscade.

## N° 55        GOLDEN SLIPPER
### Verre F

Prendre un petit verre F, verser quart de chartreuse jaune, mettre délicatement un jaune d'œuf entier bien frais, puis remplir le verre tout doucement avec de l'eau-de-vie de Dantzig et servir.

C'est une des boissons les plus favorites de nos Américaines.

## N° 56        "LUCY" POUSSE-CAFE
### Verre G

Prendre un petit verre G flûte, le remplir moitié chartreuse jaune, moitié cognac Curlier, en ayant soin de ne pas mélanger et servir.

## N° 57        KNICKERBEIN
### Verre D

Prendre un verre à Cocktail D, verser un quart de crème de vanille un jaune d'œuf entier, le couvrir légèrement d'une couche de bénédictine. Remplir le verre avec du kummel, 2 traits d'angostura et servir.

Il est indispensable de verser bien doucement toutes ces liqueurs, afin de ne pas les mélanger.

### Nº 58 LOUIS' KNICKERBEIN

#### Verre D

Prendre un verre à Cocktail D, verser quart de marasquin, déposer délicatement un jaune d'œuf entier, puis remplir le verre en versant doucement curaçao, kirsch et cognac Curlier, en laissant un léger faux-col. Battre le blanc de l'œuf avec un batteur et lorsque le blanc est devenu presque solide, le verser légèrement en pyramide sur le verre et arroser de 2 traits de curaçao pour décorer et servir.

Il est préférable de mélanger à cette crème un peu de sucre ou de vanille, afin de parfumer et flatter le palais.

### Nº 59 KNICKERBOCKER

#### Verre C

Prendre gobelet argent, glace en petits morceaux, une petite cuillerée de jus de citron, 2 cuillerées de sirop de framboises, 4 traits de curaçao, finir avec rhum vieux et eau, bien frapper, passer, verser et servir.

### Nº 60 LADIES BLUSH

#### Verre C

Prendre gobelet argent, glace en morceaux, un petit verre à liqueur d'anisette Cusenier, 2 traits de curaçao, finir avec absinthe blanche et eau, frapper fortement, passer, verser et servir.

N° 61                    **LAST DRINK**

VERRE ROUGE F

Prendre le verre à mélange A pour Cocktail, glace en petits morceaux et verser en quantité égale : cognac Curlier, chartreuse jaune, cherry brandy, ginger brandy, kummel OO; bien agiter, passer, verser dans un petit verre rouge F, dont vous aurez sucré les bords comme l'indique page 7, et servir.

Cette boisson est la consommation la plus appréciée des Américains après un bon repas.

N° 62                **LEAVE IT TO ME**

VERRE C

Prendre gobelet argent, glace en petits morceaux, une petite cuillerée de sucre poudre, jus d'un demi-citron, une cuillerée à bouche de sirop de framboises, une cuillerée à bouche de marasquin, finir avec du old tom gin, bien frapper, passer, verser, une tranche de citron et servir.

N° 63                  **MINUIT 30**

VERRE C

Prendre gobelet argent, glace en petits morceaux, une cuillerée à café de bon miel, 4 traits de curaçao, finir avec scotch whisky et vin rouge de Bourgogne, bien frapper, passer, verser et servir.

N° 64                  **MAGNOLIA**

VERRE C

Prendre gobelet argent, glace en morceaux, 1 jaune d'œuf, 1 verre à liqueur de fine champagne Curlier, une cuillerée à café de marasquin, une cuillerée à café de sucre poudre, frapper fortement, passer, verser. Remplir le verre avec du champagne Sillery sec Henriot, remuer légèrement avec la cuillère et servir.

### N° 65        MAIDEN'S BLUSH
#### Verre C

Prendre un gobelet argent, glace en morceaux, demi cuillerée de sucre poudre, une cuillerée de sirop de framboises, jus d'un demi-citron, 1 verre à liqueur d'absinthe blanche, 1 demi-verre de old tom gin, finir avec un peu d'eau, frapper, passer, verser, tranche de citron et servir.

### N° 66        MORNING CALL
#### Verre C

Prendre gobelet argent, glace en petits morceaux, une petite cuillerée de sucre poudre, 6 traits de curaçao, 4 traits d'angostura, finir avec rhum ou cognac Curlier et eau en quantité égale, bien frapper, passer, verser, couper un zeste de citron en spirale et servir.

Cette boisson est recommandée le matin au saut du lit.

### N° 67        NIGHT CAP (BONNET DE NUIT)
#### Verre rouge E

Prendre gobelet argent, glace en morceaux, une cuillerée de sucre poudre et verser en quantité égale punch au rhum doux, cognac Curlier et eau, frapper, passer, verser et servir.

# AUX OLIVIERS

## d'AIX et de NICE

### 66, Chaussée d'Antin - PARIS

---

## ḥUILE D'OLIVE VIERGE

### ḥuile Bourgeoise

## VINAIGRE D'ORLÉANS

### Eau de fleur d'Oranger

## SAVON BLANC PUR

---

✣ Livraison à domicile ✣

✣ Expédition en Province ✣

N° 68                  ## PRAIERIE OYSTER

Verre D

Boisson recommandée pour préparer l'estomac avant un bon repas.

Prendre un verre D, casser un œuf, y déposer délicatement le jaune, sel, poivre de Cayenne, sauce anglaise, quelques gouttes de bon vinaigre, finir avec sherry et cognac Curlier en quantité égale et servir. Il faut boire cette consommation autant que possible d'un seul trait.


N° 69             ## PICK ME UP (RAMASSE-MOI)

Verre C

Prendre un gobelet en argent, glace en morceaux, une cuillerée à bouche de jus de citron, une cuillerée à bouche de grenadine, une cuillerée à bouche de kirsch vieux, bien frapper, passer, verser. Remplir le verre avec du champagne Henriot, Sillery sec, ajouter demi-tranche orange, agiter légèrement avec la cuillère et servir.


N° 70                 ## POUSSE L'AMOUR

Verre rouge F

Prendre un verre rouge F, une cuillerée à café de marasquin, casser un œuf, y mettre délicatement le jaune entier, 4 traits de curaçao, 4 traits de crème de noyaux, finir avec du cognac Curlier et servir sans mélanger.

Cette boisson doit être avalée d'un trait.

### N° 71      POUSSE-CAFÉ
#### Verre G

Prendre un verre flûte G, y verser, au moyen du dos d'une cuillère, sans mélanger et en quantité égale : anisette, menthe verte, cherry brandy, fine champagne Curlier et servir.

### N° 72      POUSSE-CAFÉ PARISIEN
#### Verre G

Se fait de la même manière que la recette précédente, mais avec 3 liqueurs : curaçao, kirsch, chartreuse.

### N° 73      PORT FLIP
#### Verre C

Prendre gobelet argent, glace en morceaux, 4 traits de curaçao, 2 traits de crème de noyaux, une petite cuillerée de sucre poudre, 1 jaune d'œuf bien frais, finir avec du Porto rouge, frapper fortement, passer, verser, saupoudrer de muscade et servir.

### N° 74      QUEEN CHARLOTTE
#### Verre C

Prendre gobelet argent, glace en morceaux, une cuillerée et demie de sirop de groseille, 1 verre à liqueur de fine champagne, 3 traits de crème de noyaux, 2 traits de curaçao, une petite cuillerée de crème de menthe, bien frapper, passer, verser, finir avec de l'eau de seltz, une tranche d'orange et servir.

No 75 ## SQUARE MEAL
### Verre rouge E

Prendre gobelet argent, glace en morceaux, un jaune d'œuf bien frais, 3 traits de curaçao, 2 traits de crème de noyaux, demi-verre à liqueur de ginger brandy, finir avec fine champagne, bien frapper, passer, verser et servir.

No 76 ## SAM WARD
### Verre D

Prendre un verre à Cocktail D, le remplir de glace pilée, verser de la chartreuse jaune, couper un long zeste de citron et le glisser entre le verre et la glace, une cerise à l'eau-de-vie et servir avec chalumeaux.

Il y a beaucoup d'américains qui font ajouter une petite cuillerée de menthe verte avant de servir.

No 77 ## SHERRY FLIP
### Verre C

Prendre gobelet argent, glace en morceaux, 4 traits de curaçao, 2 traits de crème de noyaux, une petite cuillerée de sucre en poudre, 1 jaune d'œuf bien frais, finir avec du sherry, frapper fortement, passer, verser, saupoudrer de muscade et servir.

No 78 ## SHERRY AND EGG
### Verre jaune E

Prendre un verre à pied jaune E, casser un œuf bien frais, y mettre délicatement le jaune, remplir de sherry sec Sanderman et servir.

| N° 79 | ## STARS AND STRIPES |

### Verre G

Cette boisson, qui signifie les Étoiles et les Raies, se sert de la manière suivante :

Verser dans le verre G, successivement et sans mélanger, crème de noyaux rouge, marasquin, chartreuse jaune, curaçao vert, fine champagne Curlier.

Voilà pour les Raies; maintenant pour les Étoiles, buvez le contenu du verre d'un seul coup, payez et sortez, vous verrez les étoiles. C'est à ce moment que le propriétaire est heureux de fermer ses portes, lorsqu'il a des clients par trop ennuyeux, en raison de l'heure tardive.

| N° 80 | ## SILVER FIZZ |

### Verre C

Prendre gobelet argent, glace en morceaux, 2 cuillerées à café de sucre poudre, 1 blanc d'œuf bien frais, 2 verres à liqueur de vieux gin, bien frapper, passer, verser. Remplir avec de l'eau de seltz, demi-tranche de citron et servir.

| N° 81 | ## THUNDER |

### Verre jaune E

Le Tonnerre se sert de la manière suivante :

Prendre gobelet argent, glace en petits morceaux, demi-cuillerée de sucre poudre, 1 œuf entier bien frais, 1 verre à liqueur de cognac Curlier et une forte pincée de poivre de Cayenne, bien frapper, passer, verser et servir.

# ALBERT ROGER

## FROMAGES EN GROS

### SPÉCIALITÉ
DE

## Chester Anglais & Canadien, Cheddar
### STILTON et HOLLANDE
de provenance directe

## GROS — DEMI-GROS

## COMMISSION — EXPORTATION

*38, Rue des Bourdonnais, 38*

# PARIS

TÉLÉPHONE No 128-75

## N° 82  TOO-TOO
### Verre C

Prendre gobelet argent, glace, une petite cuillerée de sucre poudre, 1 œuf bien frais, une cuillerée à bouche de sirop de framboises, finir avec cognac Curlier et rhum, frapper fortement, passer, verser et servir.

## N° 83  WHISKEY SOUR
### Verre C

Prendre gobelet argent, glace en petits morceaux, une petite cuillerée de sucre en poudre, 2 cuillerées à bouche de jus de citron. Remplir avec eau et scotch whisky en quantité égale, frapper, passer, verser, demi-tranche de citron et servir.

## N° 84  WHISKEY FLASH
### Verre rouge C

Prendre gobelet argent, glace en morceaux, une cuillerée de sucre poudre, une cuillerée à bouche de jus de citron, 2 cuillerées à bouche de sirop d'ananas, finir avec scotch whisky et eau en quantité égale, frapper fortement, passer, verser et servir.

## N° 85  WHISKEY CRUSTA
### Verre jaune E

Prendre gobelet argent, glace en morceaux, une cuillerée à bouche de sirop de gomme, 2 traits d'orange bitter, 2 traits de jus de citron, 4 traits de marasquin, finir avec du scotch whisky, bien frapper, passer et servir dans le verre E, dont on aura eu soin de sucrer les bords auparavant, en les passant d'abord légèrement dans le jus de citron et dans le sucre en ensuite.

### Nº 86     WHISKEY DAISY L'AMOUR
#### Verre C

Prendre gobelet argent, glace en morceaux, une petite cuillerée de sucre poudre, 2 cuillerées à bouche de jus de citron, 4 traits de sirop de framboises, finir avec scotch whisky et siphon, bien frapper, passer, verser et servir.

### Nº 87     WHISKEY FLIP
#### Verre B

Prendre gobelet en argent, glace en morceaux, 3 traits de curaçao, 3 traits de noyaux, 1 jaune d'œuf bien frais, une cuillerée de sucre poudre, finir avec du scotch ou irish whisky, bien frapper, passer, verser, saupoudrer de muscade et servir.

# TROISIÈME PARTIE

---

## LES

# COBBLERS, PUNCHS

## ETC.

### et leurs

# PRÉPARATIONS

---

Fouquet's staff circa 1900
(*left*) and its façade circa 1925
(*opposite*).

# TROISIÈME PARTIE

# COBBLERS, PUNCHS

Les Cobblers et les Punchs demandent un grand soin à préparer. Le Cobbler est une boisson très populaire en Amérique, et est très à la mode durant l'été. Le Cobbler peut être composé de sherry, whisky, brandy, champagne, etc. Comme toutes les autres boissons, c'est aux Américains que nous devons ces précieuses mixtures qui sont maintenant très appréciées et recherchées dans tous les climats chauds. Leur préparation demande un très grand soin, afin de flatter à la fois l'œil et le palais. Il est nécessaire d'y apporter un raffinement tout particulier pour orner les verres. Presque tous les Cobblers et les Punchs sont à peu près la même chose et ne diffèrent les uns des autres que par la liqueur avec laquelle ils sont faits, la base des essences étant presque toujours la même.

Pendant la bonne saison, il faut toujours autant que possible garnir les verres de fruits les plus parfumés, que vous remplacerez en hiver par l'ananas et les fruits à l'eau-de-vie.

Dans cette partie, vous trouverez aussi toutes les boissons fraîches, comme citronnade, orangeade, etc.

Toutes ces consommations doivent être faites directement dans les verres qui doivent être servis sans avoir recours pour les mélanger aux gobelets en argent.

Quelques-unes, cependant, font exception à la règle, comme vous le verrez du reste dans mes recettes.

Il est bon de se munir d'une passoire à boisson, afin de passer la glace pour les personnes ne désirant pas boire au moyen des chalumeaux.

**Passoire à boisson**
Pièce **18** fr.

# USTENSILES A PILER LA GLACE
## POUR COBBLERS & PUNCHS

**Seau pour la Glace à rafraichir**

| Petit... | Haut 0ᵐ10 | Pièce 14 fr. |
|---|---|---|
| Moyen.. | » 0ᵐ12 | » 17 » |
| Grand.. | » 0ᵐ14 | » 42 » |

**Pelle pour la Glace**
Pièce. ........ 6 fr.

**Machine à casser la glace** (nickelée)
Pièce...... 50 fr.

**Couteau pique-glace**
Pièce  5 fr.

**Passoire à boisson**
Pièce... 18 fr.

N° 88       **AMERICAN LEMONADE**

Verre B

Remplir de glace pilée verre B, 2 cuillerées à café de sucre en poudre, le jus d'un citron, remplir d'eau de seltz, bien remuer, une tranche de citron, chalumeaux, verser quelques gouttes de Porto rouge sans mélanger et servir.

N° 89       **ALE PUNCH**

Verre B

Remplir à moitié de glace pilée verre B, jus d'un demi-citron, verser pale ale, vin blanc et cognac Curlier en quantité égale, bien remuer et, au moment de servir, saupoudrer de muscade et garnir de 2 zestes de citron, chalumeaux.

N° 90       **BRANDY SLING**

Verre B

Remplir de glace pilée verre B, 2 cuillerées de sucre poudre, jus d'un citron, 1 verre à madère de cognac Curlier, finir avec de l'eau de seltz, bien remuer, chalumeaux et servir.

N° 91       **BRANDY PUNCH**

Verre B

Remplir de glace pilée verre B, une petite cuillerée de sucre poudre, 3 traits d'angostura, 4 traits de curaçao, 2 traits de noyaux, remplir de cognac vieux, bien remuer, 1 zeste de citron, chalumeaux et servir.

## Nᵒ 92  BRANDY SMASH
### Verre B

Remplir de glace pilée verre B, une petite cuillerée de sucre poudre, 4 traits de curaçao, 4 traits de noyaux, finir avec cognac Curlier et eau en quantité égale, bien remuer, saupoudrer de muscade, chalumeaux et servir.

## Nᵒ 93  BRANDY COBBLER
### Verre B

Remplir de glace pilée verre B, 2 cuillerées à café de sucre poudre, 3 traits de curaçao, 3 traits de noyaux, remplir avec cognac Curlier, bien remuer, glisser le long du verre une tranche orange, une tranche citron, fruits frais ou cerises à l'eau-de-vie, chalumeaux, quelques gouttes de Porto rouge sans agiter et servir.

## Nᵒ 94  BRUNSWICK COOLER
### Verre A

Prendre un grand verre A, remplir de glace pilée, le jus d'un citron, 2 cuillerées à bouche de sucre poudre, verser une bouteille de ginger ale, bien remuer, une tranche de citron, fruits, chalumeaux et servir.

## Nᵒ 95  BITTER HAVRAIS
### Verre B

Prendre verre B, verser un verre à liqueur de cognac, puis le bitter, piler un morceau de sucre au fond du verre au moyen d'une cuillère à pilon. Remplir avec de l'eau de seltz, bien agiter.

Nº 96      **CRITERION LEMONADE**

VERRE B

Remplir de glace pilée verre B, 3 cuillerées à café sucre poudre, jus d'un demi-citron, une cuillerée à bouche de sirop de framboises, finir avec de l'eau pure, bien remuer, une tranche de citron, fruits, chalumeaux, 1 trait de Porto rouge Sandeman sans mélanger et servir.

Nº 97      **CHAMPAGNE CUP**

VERRE B

Remplir de glace pilée verre B, 3 traits de curaçao, 2 traits de noyaux, une cuillerée à café de marasquin, finir avec du champagne goût américain Henriot, bien remuer, chalumeaux, et au moment de servir, verser doucement quelques gouttes de cherry brandy sans mélanger.

Nº 98      **CLARET CUP**

VERRE B

Remplir de glace pilée verre B, 2 cuillerées à café de sucre poudre, 3 traits de curaçao, 3 traits de noyaux, une cuillerée à café de marasquin, presser demi-citron, finir avec du bordeaux rouge vieux, bien remuer, une tranche orange, chalumeaux et servir.

Nº 99      **LOUIS CLARET CUP**

VERRE B

Remplir de glace pilée verre B, une cuillerée à café de sucre poudre, 2 traits de curaçao, 2 traits de noyaux, un demi-verre à liqueur de kirsch vieux, finir avec bon bordeaux rouge et champagne Henriot, Sillery doux, bien remuer, une tranche orange, chalumeaux et servir.

# CHAMPAGNE
# HENRIOT
### Successeur de
## AUGER-GODINOT

*Maison fondée en 1808*

## REIMS

---

## PRIX-COURANT

*Franco en Gare dans toute la France*

---

| | | |
|---|---|---|
| "Souverain" Extra Qualité...... | 7.50 | |
| Carte Blanche................ | 6.75 | |
| Verzenay Supérieur.. .......... | 6 | » |
| Sillery Supérieur....... ........ | 5 | )) |
| Sillery Première qualité.......... | 4 | » |

0 fr. 50 en plus pour $^2/_2$ bouteilles

*Paiement à 3 mois sans escompte ou à 30 jours 2 0/0*

---

### Agent à Paris :

M. Albert VAVASSEUR, 31, Avenue de la République

N° 100     ## CRITERION REFRESHER
### Verre B

Remplir de glace pilée verre B, 3 traits d'angostura, finir avec moitié vermouth de Turin, moitié vieux gin, bien remuer, une tranche de citron, chalumeaux et servir.

N° 101     ## CHICAGO
### Verre B

Remplir de glace pilée verre B, 3 traits de noyaux, une cuillerée à bouche de grenadine, 1 verre à liqueur de cognac Curlier, finir avec moitié amer Besset, moitié eau de seltz, bien remuer, une tranche de citron et servir avec chalumeaux.

N° 102     ## CHAMPAGNE COBBLER
### Verre B

Remplir de glace pilée verre B, 3 traits de curaçao, 3 traits de crème de noyaux, finir avec du champagne Henriot, Sillery doux, bien remuer, une tranche orange, une tranche citron, fruits selon la saison, chalumeaux, 2 traits de Porto rouge Sandeman sans mélanger et servir.

N° 103     ## CLARET PUNCH
### Verre B

Remplir de glace pilée verre B, 3 traits de curaçao, 3 traits de crème de noyaux, 2 cuillerées de sucre poudre, finir avec du bordeaux rouge vieux, bien remuer, une tranche d'orange, chalumeaux et servir.

**N° 104**       # COFFEE PUNCH
### Verre B

Remplir de glace pilée verre B, 2 traits de curaçao, 2 traits de noyaux, 2 cuillerées de sucre poudre, 1 verre à liqueur de cognac Curlier, rhum ou kirsch au goût de la personne, finir avec du café, bien remuer, chalumeaux et servir.

**N° 105**       # CRITERION'S OWN PUNCH
### Verre B

Remplir à moitié de glace pilée verre B, 2 traits curaçao, 2 traits de crème de noyaux, 2 cuillerées de sucre poudre, 1 jaune d'œuf bien frais, finir avec du café, frapper en ajustant un gobelet en argent sur votre verre et secouer de haut en bas; attendre quelques minutes, découvrir doucement pour ne pas faire tomber la mousse en dehors du verre, chalumeaux et servir.

**N° 106**       # CURAÇAO PUNCH
### Verre B

Remplir de glace pilée verre B, 2 cuillerées de sucre poudre, presser demi-citron, 1 verre à liqueur de cognac Curlier, 1 verre à liqueur de rhum, 1 verre à madère de curaçao, finir avec de l'eau, bien remuer, une tranche d'orange, fruits selon la saison, chalumeaux et servir.

**N° 107**       # CANADIEN PUNCH
### Verre B

Remplir de glace pilée, 2 cuillerées de sucre poudre, 3 traits de curaçao, 3 traits de noyaux, 1 verre à liqueur de rhum, une cuillerée à bouche de jus de citron, finir avec de l'eau et du rye whisky en quantité égale, bien remuer, une tranche citron, une tranche ananas, chalumeaux et servir.

## N° 108    COSMOPOLITAN CLARET PUNCH
### Verre B

Remplir de glace pilée verre B, 3 traits de curaçao, 2 traits de noyaux, 2 cuillerées de sucre poudre, 1 verre à liqueur de cognac Curlier. Remplir et finir avec du bordeaux rouge, une tranche d'orange, fruits selon la saison, chalumeaux et servir.

## N° 109    CIDER PUNCH
### Verre B

Remplir de glace pilée verre B, 2 cuillerées de sucre poudre, 1 verre à madère de sherry sec, 1 verre à liqueur de cognac Curlier, presser le jus d'un demi-citron, finir avec du cidre, bien remuer, une tranche d'orange, 2 zestes de citron, fruits selon la saison, chalumeaux et servir.

Beaucoup d'américains font un Cider Punch avec du cognac, dans lequel ils ont fait macérer pendant quelques jours plusieurs pelures de concombres, pour donner un parfum délicat et recherché.

## N° 110    CIDER CUP
### Verre B

Remplir de glace pilée verre B, 3 traits de curaçao, 3 traits de crème de noyaux, une cuillerée à café de sucre poudre, finir avec du bon cidre et champagne Henriot en égale quantité, bien remuer, une tranche d'orange, fruits selon la saison, chalumeaux et servir.

### N° 111     CALIFORNIA WINE COBBLER
#### Verre B

Remplir de glace pilée verre B, 2 traits de curaçao, une cuillerée de sucre en poudre, presser le jus d'une orange, remplir avec du vin de Californie, bien remuer, 2 traits de Porto rouge Sandeman sans mélanger, chalumeaux et servir.

### N° 112     EGG NOG
#### Verre B

Remplir à moitié de glace pilée verre B, 2 traits de noyaux, 2 traits de curaçao, 2 cuillerées de sucre poudre, 1 jaune d'œuf bien frais, finir avec lait et sherry Sandeman en quantité égale, ajuster sur votre verre un gobelet en argent et bien frapper, chalumeaux et servir.

### N° 113     EGG LEMONADE
#### Verre B

Remplir à moitié de glace pilée verre B, jus d'un demi-citron, une cuillerée de sucre en poudre, 1 œuf bien frais, ajuster sur votre verre un gobelet en argent et bien frapper. Remplir ensuite avec de l'eau de seltz ou du soda, remuer, chalumeaux et servir.

### N° 114     FISHERMAN'S PRAYER
#### (LA PRIÈRE DES PÊCHEURS)
#### Verre B

Remplir de glace pilée verre B, une cuillerée de sucre poudre, presser demi-citron, 1 verre à liqueur de sirop de framboises, 1 verre à liqueur de bon rhum, finir avec de l'eau, bien remuer, fruits selon la saison, chalumeaux et servir.

N° 115      ## GIN SLING
### Verre B

Remplir de glace pilée verre B, 2 cuillerées de sucre poudre, 1 verre à liqueur de vieux gin, presser le jus d'un citron. Remplir avec de l'eau pure, bien remuer, chalumeaux et servir.

N° 116      ## GIN AND MILK (LAIT ET GIN)
### Verre B

Remplir de glace pilée verre B, une cuillerée de sirop de gomme, 2 traits de crème de noyaux, finir avec gin et lait en quantité égale, bien remuer, chalumeaux et servir.

N° 117      ## GIN PUNCH
### Verre B

Remplir de glace pilée verre B, 2 traits de crème de noyaux, une cuillerée à bouche de sirop de framboises, 2 cuillerées de sucre poudre, finir avec gin et eau pure en quantité égale, bien remuer, une tranche d'orange, une tranche d'ananas, chalumeaux et servir.

N° 118      ## GLASGOW FLIP
### Verre A

Remplir à moitié de glace pilée un grand verre A, 1 œuf bien frais, le jus d'un citron, une cuillerée de sucre en poudre. Remplir avec une bouteille de ginger ale, bien remuer, chalumeaux et servir.

### N° 119     HORSE GUARDS BISHOP
#### Verre B

Remplir de glace pilée verre B, 4 traits de curaçao, finir avec rhum et champagne Sillery Henriot supérieur en quantité égale, bien remuer et faire tremper dans le verre une pelure de citron très mince découpée en spirale, chalumeaux et servir.

### N° 120     ICE CREAM SODA
#### Verre B

Remplir de glace pilée verre B, 2 traits de crème de noyaux, demi-verre à liqueur de kirsch, 1 verre à liqueur de crème de vanille, finir avec lait et eau de seltz en quantité égale, bien remuer, chalumeaux et servir.

### N° 121     ICED COFFEE (CAFE GLACÉ)
#### Verre B

Remplir de glace pilée verre B, 2 traits de crème de noyaux, demi-verre de cognac Curlier ou de rhum au goût du client, remplir de café, 2 cuillerées de sucre poudre, adapter gobelet argent et frapper fortement; attendre quelques minutes et servir avec toute la mousse, chalumeaux.

### N° 122     ICED TEA (THÉ GLACÉ)
#### Verre B

Remplir de glace pilée verre B, 2 traits crème de noyaux, demi-verre à liqueur de rhum, 2 cuillerées sucre poudre, finir avec du thé froid, adapter gobelet argent et frapper fortement; attendre quelques minutes et servir avec toute la mousse en y ajoutant 2 tranches d'orange et chalumeaux.

# USTENSILES POUR LES BOISSONS AU CITRON

**Presse-Citron**
(nickelé)

Pièce........ **80** fr.

**Presse à Citron** entièrement en métal blanc (argenté)   Pièce **20** fr.

AA cuvette mobile recevant le jus du citron qui s'écoule par l'ouverture B
Modèle à gouttière   Pièce **17** fr.

**Presse-Citron** (argenté)
Pièce..... **44** fr.

Nº 123        JOHN COLLINS
VERRE B

Remplir de glace pilée verre B, 2 cuillerées de sucre poudre, presser un citron, 1 verre à liqueur de gin, finir avec de l'eau de seltz ou soda, bien remuer, 1 rond de citron, chalumeaux et servir.

Nº 124        LEMON AND DASH
VERRE A

Prendre verre A, 1 morceau de glace, verser 3/4 de limonade gazeuse, remplir avec allsopp's pale ale, une pelure de citron coupée en spirale et servir.

Nº 125        LEMON SQUASH (CITRONNADE)
VERRE B

Remplir de glace pilée verre B, 2 cuillerées de sucre poudre, presser un citron, finir avec de l'eau de seltz ou soda, bien remuer, une tranche de citron, chalumeaux et servir.

Nº 126        MILK PUNCH (PUNCH AU LAIT FROID)
VERRE B

Remplir de glace verre B, 2 traits de noyaux, 2 cuillerées sucre poudre, demi-verre à liqueur de cognac Curlier, demi-verre à liqueur de rhum, finir avec du lait, adapter gobelet argent, frapper fortement; attendre quelques minutes, servir avec toute la mousse, saupoudrer de muscade, chalumeaux et servir.

MAISON FONDÉE EN 1814

# DUMINY & Cº

## AY (CHAMPAGNE)

L. GUYOT, Agent Général à Paris

*7, Rue Le Peletier, 7*

# PRIX-COURANT

|  |  | la bout. |
|---|---|---|
| Sillery Supérieur (Demi-Sec) ....... Fr. | **5** | » |
| Carte Blanche (Doux) .............. » | **6** | » |
| Carte d'Or (Sec)..... ........... ... » | **7** | » |
| Extra Dry (England)................ ...... » | **8** | » |

**FRANCO DE TOUS FRAIS A DOMICILE**

0,50 Centimes en plus par deux demi-Bouteilles

| | |
|---|---|
| CHATEAU DE CHARMIÈRES (Marque déposée), la bout. | **3.25** |
| TISANE DE CHAMPAGNE .............. » | **3.25** |

## Nᵒ 127    MOTHER'S MILK (LAIT DE MÈRE)
### Verre B

Remplir de glace pilée verre B, 3 traits de curaçao, 2 traits de noyaux, une cuillerée à bouche de grenadine, 1 jaune d'œuf bien frais, 1 verre à liqueur de cognac Curlier, finir avec du lait, adapter gobelet argent, frapper fortement; attendre quelques minutes, servir avec la mousse, chalumeaux, saupoudrer de muscade.

## Nᵒ 128    MISSISSIPPI PUNCH
### Verre B

Remplir de glace pilée verre B, 2 cuillerées sucre poudre, 3 traits de jus de citron, 1 verre à liqueur de cognac Curlier, 1 verre à liqueur de rhum, 1 verre à liqueur de bourbon whisky, finir avec de l'eau de seltz ou soda, bien remuer, fruits selon la saison, une tranche de citron, chalumeaux et servir.

## Nᵒ 129    ORANGEADE
### Verre B

Remplir de glace pilée verre B, 2 cuillerées de sucre poudre, 1 verre à liqueur de curaçao, presser le jus d'une orange, finir avec de l'eau pure, bien remuer, une tranche d'orange, chalumeaux et servir.

## Nᵒ 130    ORGEAT LEMONADE
### Verre B

Remplir de glace pilée verre B, une cuillerée de sucre poudre, jus d'un demi-citron, 1 verre à liqueur de sirop d'orgeat, finir avec de l'eau pure, bien remuer, une tranche de citron, fruits selon la saison, chalumeaux, 4 traits de sirop de framboises et servir sans mélanger.

### N° 131     ORGEAT PUNCH
#### Verre B

Remplir de glace pilée verre B, 2 traits de crème de noyaux, 1 verre à liqueur de cognac Curlier, finir avec orgeat et eau pure, bien remuer, une tranche de citron, fruits selon la saison, chalumeaux et 2 traits de Porto rouge avant de servir.

### N° 132     OLD CHUM'S REVIVER
#### Verre B

Remplir de glace pilée verre B, jus d'un demi-citron, une cuillerée de sucre poudre, 1 verre à liqueur de cognac Curlier, finir avec sirop de fraises et eau de seltz, ou soda, bien remuer, cerises à l'eau-de-vie, chalumeaux et servir.

### N° 133     PORT SANGAREE
#### Verre B

Remplir de glace pilée verre B, 2 traits de curaçao, une cuillerée de sucre poudre, finir avec Porto rouge Sandeman et eau pure en quantité égale, bien remuer, saupoudrer de muscade, chalumeaux et servir.

### N° 134     PRINCE OF WALES (PRINCE DE GALLES)
#### Verre B

Remplir de glace pilée verre B, 3 traits de curaçao, 2 traits de noyaux, 1 verre à madère de madère sec, une cuillerée de sucre poudre et finir avec du champagne Henriot sec et eau de seltz ou soda; bien remuer, une tranche de citron, chalumeaux, 2 traits de cherry brandy et servir sans mélanger.

Nº 135    PUNCH A LA ROMAINE
VERRE B

Remplir de glace pilée verre B, 4 traits de curaçao, une cuillerée de sucre poudre, 2 traits de jus de citron, 1 œuf bien frais, une cuillerée à café de rhum vieux, finir avec du vin de Bordeaux blanc; adapter gobelet argent et frapper fortement, chalumeaux, saupoudrer de muscade et servir.

Nº 136    PHILADELPHIA BOATING PUNCH
VERRE B

Remplir de glace pilée verre B, 2 cuillerées de sucre en poudre, jus d'un demi-citron, 1 verre à liqueur de rhum, 1 verre à liqueur de cognac Curlier, finir avec de l'eau pure, bien remuer, fruits de la saison, une tranche de citron, chalumeaux et servir.

Nº 137    RUM PUNCH COLD
VERRE B

Remplir de glace pilée verre B, 3 traits de curaçao, 3 traits de noyaux, 2 cuillerées de sucre poudre, finir avec rhum vieux et eau pure, bien remuer, saupoudrer de muscade, chalumeaux et servir.

Nº 138        **RANSOM COOLER**

VERRE B

Remplir de glace pilée verre B, 3 traits de noyaux, 4 traits de curaçao, une cuillerée à bouche de grenadine, une cuillerée à bouche de kirsch vieux, finir avec moitié amer moitié eau de seltz; bien remuer, une tranche de citron, chalumeaux et servir.

Nº 139        **ROCKY MOUNTAIN PUNCH**

VERRE B

Remplir de glace pilée verre B, 2 cuillerées de sucre poudre, presser demi-citron, demi-verre de rhum Jamaïque, une cuillerée à bouche de marasquin, finir avec du champagne Henriot, goût anglais, bien remuer, une tranche de citron, fruits selon la saison, 1 morceau de sucre candie, chalumeaux et servir.

Nº 140        **ROMAN PUNCH**

VERRE B

Remplir de glace pilée verre B, une cuillerée à café de sucre poudre, 3 traits de jus de citron, presser le jus d'une demi-orange, 1 verre à liqueur de curaçao, 1 verre et demi à liqueur de rhum vieux, finir avec cognac, bien remuer, fruits selon la saison, chalumeaux, 2 traits de porto rouge Sandeman sans mélanger et servir.

# Bouteilles & Bouchons

*Établissement fondé en 1795*

# EDARD

| PARIS | | LONDRES |
|---|---|---|
| **26 et 28, r. du Dragon** | **E. MELIN,** Succes. | **9, Morgan's Lane, 9** |
| (Faub. St-Germain) | TÉLÉPHONE | (S. E.) |

## SPÉCIALITÉ DE BOUTEILLES MOULÉES
### Pour Vins d'Espagne et Spiritueux Anglais

### SEUL DÉPOT DES VERRERIES
de **VAUXROT** (Aisne), **LOURCHES** (Nord), **ARQUES** (Pas-de-Calais)

## CHAMPAGNE STAND

COGNAC          PORTO          MADÈRE          KIRSCH

# USTENSILES POUR LE DÉBOUCHAGE DES BOUTEILLES

**Tire-Bouchon** mécanique
(petit)

Pièce............... **30 fr.**

**Grand Tire-Bouchon** (nickelé)

Pièce..... **80 fr.**

Nᵒ 141 **RHINE WINE COBBLER**
**(COBBLER AU VIN DU RHIN)**
Verre B

Remplir de glace pilée verre B, une cuillerée à café de sucre poudre, 3 traits de curaçao, 2 traits de noyaux, finir avec vin du Rhin et eau en égale quantité, bien remuer, fruits selon la saison, une tranche d'ananas, une tranche d'orange. chalumeaux et servir.

N. B. — Cette boisson est très en vogue en Allemagne,

Nᵒ 142 **ROCKY MOUNTAIN COOLER**
Verre B

Remplir à moitié de glace pilée verre B, 1 œuf bien frais, une cuillerée de sucre poudre, jus d'un citron, finir avec du bon cidre, bien frapper en ajustant gobelet argent, chalumeaux, saupoudrer de muscade et servir.

Nᵒ 143 **SHERRY SANGAREE**
Verre B

Remplir de glace pilée verre B, 3 traits de curaçao, 2 traits de noyaux, une cuillerée de sucre poudre, finir avec du sherry Sandeman, bien remuer, chalumeaux, saupoudrer de muscade et servir.

Nᵒ 144 **SOYER AU CHAMPAGNE**
Verre B

Remplir de glace pilée verre B, 3 traits de curaçao, demi-verre à liqueur de marasquin; remplir de champagne Jules

Mumm dry, bien remuer, chalumeaux et au moment de servir, verser sans mélanger quelques gouttes de bonne crème de vanille.

**Nᵒ 145**

## SHERRY COBBLER
### Verre B

Remplir de glace pilée verre B, 2 traits de noyaux, 2 traits de curaçao, 2 cuillerées à café de sucre poudre, finir avec du sherry Sandeman, bien remuer, 1 rond d'orange, 1 rond de citron, fruits de la saison, chalumeaux et au moment de servir, verser doucement un peu de porto rouge sans mélanger.

**Nᵒ 146**

## SANTA CRUZ PUNCH
### Verre B

Remplir de glace pilée verre B, 2 traits de curaçao, 2 traits de noyaux, une cuillerée de sucre en poudre, finir avec rhum vieux et eau, bien remuer, une tranche de citron, chalumeaux et servir.

**Nᵒ 147**

## SARATOGA COOLER
### Verre A

Remplir à moitié de glace pilée verre A, une cuillerée de sucre poudre, jus d'un demi-citron, verser une bouteille de ginger ale, bien remuer, chalumeaux et servir.

**Nᵒ 148**

## SAUTERNE PUNCH
### Verre B

Remplir de glace pilée verre B, une cuillerée de sucre poudre, 3 traits de curaçao, finir avec du vin de Sauternes

(Château Peyron), bien agiter, une tranche d'orange, une tranche de citron, demi-tranche d'ananas, chalumeaux, fruits selon la saison et servir.

N⁰ 149          ## STONE FENCE
### VERRE B

Remplir de glace pilée verre B, 3 traits de sirop de gomme, 1 verre à liqueur de cognac Curlier, remplir avec du cidre doux, bien remuer, chalumeaux et servir.

N⁰ 150          ## TIP-TOP PUNCH
### VERRE B

Remplir de glace pilée verre B, presser demi-citron, 1 verre à liqueur de bon cognac Curlier; remplir avec du champagne Henriot, carte blanche, bien remuer, une tranche d'orange, une tranche d'ananas, fruits selon la saison, chalumeaux et servir.

N⁰ 151          ## VANILLA PUNCH
### VERRE B

Remplir de glace pilée verre B, 2 traits de curaçao, 2 traits de noyaux, moitié crème de vanille, moitié eau, bien remuer, une tranche d'orange, chalumeaux et servir.

N⁰ 152          ## WHISKEY SLING
### VERRE B

Remplir de glace pilée verre B, 2 cuillerées de sucre poudre, presser le jus d'un citron, 1 verre à liqueur de scotch whisky, finir avec de l'eau de seltz ou soda, bien remuer, chalumeaux et servir.

# GRAND VIN DE SAUTERNES
# CHÂTEAU PEYRON

### MIS EN BOUTEILLE AU CHÂTEAU

La propriété du Château Peyron a subi de très grandes trans-
formations depuis qu'elle est entre les mains de son nouveau propriétaire M. J. Charpentier, ancien négociant à Paris, dont l'unique
préoccupation est d'améliorer la qualité de nos grands vins français,
afin de maintenir leur réputation à l'étranger.

On arrive à ce résultat par des soins incessants, un travail
opiniâtre, une culture savamment faite et une vinification qui à elle
seule occasionne un travail inouï, puisqu'il faut que les raisins
soient vendangés grain par grain, etc., etc. Les vins de ce château
ont été appréciés à l'Exposition de Bordeaux l'année dernière où ils
ont obtenu la Médaille d'or, pour la première fois qu'ils figuraient à
une exposition et le propriétaire la décoration du Mérite Agricole.

Ces vins sont exquis et appelés à une grande réputation.

La récolte de l'année 1892 sera vendue à partir du mois de
Janvier 1897, au prix de **2** fr. **50** la bouteille à la propriété.

Les expéditions (minima) se font par cinq caisses de 12 bouteilles
ou bien deux caisses de 25 bouteilles.

# BASS, RATCLIFF & GRETTON Ltd

### BRASSEURS

### BURTON-ON-TRENT

# PALE ALE BURTON ALES & STOUTS

### BIÈRES RECOMMANDÉES PAR LA FACULTÉ

### EN DÉTAIL

Chez tous les Marchands de Vins et Épiciers

### EN GROS

à leur seule Succursale de France

## 152, Avenue Malakoff

# PARIS

Nº 153     **WHISKEY WHITE FLUSH**
### Verre B

Remplir de glace pilée verre B, 2 traits de curaçao, verser en quantité égale lait et rye whisky, bien remuer, chalumeaux et servir.

Nº 154     **WHISKEY SMASH**
### Verre B

Remplir de glace pilée verre B, 2 traits de curaçao, 2 traits de noyaux, une cuillerée à café de sucre poudre, finir avec du whisky (scotch ou irish), bien remuer, chalumeaux et servir.

Nº 155     **WHISKEY COBBLER**
### Verre B

Remplir de glace pilée verre B, 2 traits de curaçao, 2 traits de noyaux, 2 cuillerées à café de sucre poudre, finir avec du whisky (scotch ou irish), bien remuer, une tranche d'orange, une tranche de citron, fruits selon la saison, chalumeaux et au moment de servir verser un peu de porto rouge Sandeman sans mélanger.

Nº 156     **WHISKEY SNAPPER**
### Verre B

Remplir de glace pilée verre B, une cuillerée de sucre poudre, 4 traits de jus de citron, 2 traits de sirop de framboises, 1 verre à liqueur de scotch whisky, une petite cuillerée de miel, finir avec de l'eau de seltz ou soda, bien remuer, 1 zeste de citron, chalumeaux et servir.

### Nᵒ 157      WHISKEY STONE FENCE
#### Verre B

Remplir de glace pilée verre B, 2 cuillerées de sucre en poudre, 3 traits de sirop de gomme, 1 verre de scotch ou irish whisky, finir avec du cidre, bien remuer, chalumeaux et servir.

### Nᵒ 158      WHISKEY FIX
#### Verre B

Remplir de glace pilée verre B, 2 cuillerées de sucre en poudre, 3 traits de jus de citron, 1 verre à liqueur de scotch whisky, 1 verre et demi de sirop d'ananas, bien remuer, une tranche d'ananas, fruits selon la saison, chalumeaux et servir.

### Nᵒ 159      WHISKEY PUNCH FROID
#### Verre B

Remplir de glace pilée verre B, 3 traits de curaçao, 3 traits de noyaux, une cuillerée de sucre poudre, finir avec du scotch ou irish whisky, bien remuer, chalumeaux et servir.

# QUATRIÈME PARTIE

———

## LES

# SUMMER DRINKS

## BOISSONS D'ÉTÉ

### et leurs

# PRÉPARATIONS

———

# QUATRIÈME PARTIE

## LES

# SUMMER DRINKS

## BOISSONS D'ÉTÉ

Les Summer Drinks ne peuvent se servir que durant la bonne saison, vu les herbes et fruits frais que l'on est obligé d'employer pour leurs préparations.

Parmi ces boissons, celles qui demandent le plus d'attention et de soins sont les Juleps, c'est-à-dire toutes les boissons fabriquées avec de la menthe poivrée fraîche, que l'on pile au moyen d'une cuillère munie d'un pilon, avec un peu de sucre et d'alcool pour en extraire tout l'arôme.

Le Mint Julep est un des breuvages les plus en vogue en Amérique et les Américaines surtout en sont très amateurs pendant les plus fortes chaleurs.

Sa préparation exige un raffinement tout particulier et sa garniture, avant de servir, demande un certain goût à préparer.

En raison de la couleur que l'on obtient en préparant les Juleps, on prendra de préférence des verres rouges afin d'en masquer la couleur et de flatter le palais, et aussi très épais du fond pour résister aux chocs de la cuillère en pilant.

Pour les Punchs aux fraises et framboises, il est nécessaire de frapper fortement dans les gobelets argent avec des morceaux de glace un peu gros, afin d'écraser plus facilement les fruits, tout en en faisant sortir le parfum.

Pour les boissons aux fruits, il sera préférable d'employer aussi la passoire à boisson (page 45), afin de bien extraire jusqu'à la dernière goutte le jus que les fruits doivent rendre.

# CHAMPAGNE
# Jules MUMM

## MAISON FONDÉE EN 1827

## REIMS

———◆•◆———

## PRIX-COURANT DES VINS DE CHAMPAGNE
## JULES MUMM

Franco à domicile à Paris ou dans toute la France à la gare la plus proche

**Grand Sec** et Extra Dry Anglais fr. **8** » et fr. **8.50**
**Carte Blanche** (Doux, Sec, Demi-Sec et Dry
   Verzenay)............................... fr. **7** »
**Verzenay Cabinet** (Doux, Sec, Demi-Sec)... fr. **5** »
**Sillery Grand Mousseux** (Doux, Sec, Demi-Sec). **5.50**
**Carte Verte**............................... fr. **4.50**

0 fr. 50 en plus par $^2/_2$ bouteilles

*Expéditions de Reims en paniers de 15, 25, 30, 50 et 60 Bouteilles d'une ou plusieurs qualités, deux ½ Bouteilles comptant dans l'emballage pour une B^{lle}*

## AGENTS GÉNÉRAUX

Pour PARIS : **RENÉ EBSTEIN**, 11, Passage Saulnier

Pour la PROVINCE : **F. JOUNEAU**, 48, Rue des Abbesses, PARIS

**CUILLÈRE A PILON**

pour Juleps, Bitter Havrais, etc.

Nᵒ 160        # BRANDY JULEP
### Verre rouge B

Dans un verre rouge B, piler 3 ou 4 branches de menthe fraîche avec une cuillerée de sucre en poudre, puis 1 verre à liqueur de cognac Curlier; remplir de glace pilée, 1 verre à liqueur de chartreuse jaune, finir avec de l'eau, bien remuer, tremper dans du jus de citron une petite branche de menthe, l'ajuster au milieu du verre, chalumeaux, fruits selon la saison, 2 traits de bon cognac sans mélanger, saupoudrer le tout de sucre en poudre et servir.

Nᵒ 161        # CRITERION RUM SMASH
### Verre rouge C

Prendre gobelet argent, glace en morceaux, une cuillerée de sucre poudre, 2 branches de menthe, finir avec rhum et eau, bien frapper, passer, verser, fruits selon la saison, chalumeaux et servir.

Nᵒ 162        # CHAMPAGNE JULEP
### Verre rouge B

Dans un verre rouge B, piler 3 ou 4 branches de menthe fraîche avec une cuillerée de sucre en poudre, 1 verre à liqueur de cognac Curlier; remplir de glace pilée, 1 verre à liqueur de chartreuse jaune, finir avec du champagne Henriot sec, bien remuer, tremper dans le jus de citron une petite branche de menthe, l'ajuster au milieu du verre, chalumeaux, fruits selon la saison, 2 traits de bon rhum sans mélanger, saupoudrer le tout de sucre en poudre et servir.

## Nᵒ 163    FANCY WHISKEY SMASH
### Verre rouge C

Prendre gobelet argent, glace en morceaux, 3 brins de menthe fraîche, une cuillerée de sucre poudre, 1 verre à madère de whisky (scotch ou irish), finir avec de l'eau, bien frapper, passer, verser, fruits de la saison, chalumeaux et servir.

## Nᵒ 164    GIN JULEP
### Verre rouge B

Dans un verre rouge piler 3 ou 4 branches de menthe fraîche avec une cuillerée de sucre en poudre, puis 1 verre à liqueur de gin vieux; remplir de glace pilée, 1 verre à liqueur de chartreuse jaune, finir avec de l'eau, bien remuer, tremper dans du jus de citron une branche de menthe, l'ajuster au milieu du verre, chalumeaux, fruits de la saison, 2 traits de old tom gin sans mélanger, saupoudrer le tout de sucre en poudre et servir.

## Nᵒ 165    KILRAIN PUNCH
### Verre rouge E

Prendre gobelet argent, glace en morceaux, 3 brins de menthe fraîche, une cuillerée de sucre poudre, demi-verre à liqueur de rhum vieux, 2 cuillerées de sirop de framboises, finir avec de l'eau, bien frapper, passer, verser, fruits de la saison, 1 brin de menthe, chalumeaux et servir.

## Nᵒ 166    MINT JULEP
### Verre rouge B

Dans un verre rouge B piler 4 branches de menthe fraîche avec une cuillerée de sucre poudre, 1 verre à liqueur de

cognac Curlier; remplir de glace pilée, 1 verre à liqueur de
chartreuse jaune, finir avec de l'eau, bien remuer, tremper
dans du jus de citron une branche de menthe, l'ajuster au
milieu du verre, 3 traits de bon rhum sans mélanger, fruits,
chalumeaux, saupoudrer le tout de sucre en poudre et servir.

Nᵒ 167 ## THE PINEAPPLE JULEP
### (JULEP A L'ANANAS)
#### Verre rouge B

Dans un verre rouge B, piler 2 ou 3 brins de menthe
fraîche, jus d'une orange, une cuillerée de sirop de framboises,
une cuillerée de marasquin, une cuillerée de gin, 1 verre à
liqueur de crème d'ananas; remplir de glace pilée, finir avec
du jus d'ananas, bien remuer, tremper dans du jus de citron
une branche de menthe, l'ajuster au milieu du verre, fruits
de saison, une tranche d'ananas, chalumeaux et servir.

Nᵒ 168 ## RAPSBERRY PUNCH
### (PUNCH AUX FRAMBOISES)
#### Verre vert C

Dans gobelet argent, glace en morceaux, une douzaine
de framboises bien mûres, demi-verre de cognac Curlier,
une cuillerée à café de marasquin, une cuillerée à café de
sirop de framboises, frapper fortement, passer, verser dans
verre vert C; remplir avec du champagne Henriot Sillery
supérieur, une framboise, saupoudrer de sucre en poudre,
chalumeaux et servir.

Nᵒ 169 ## RUM JULEP
#### Verre rouge B

Se fait exactement comme le Brandy Julep, en mettant
du rhum au lieu de cognac Curlier.

Nᵒ 170 ## STRAWBERRY PUNCH
### (PUNCH AUX FRAISES)
#### Verre vert C

Dans gobelet argent, glace en morceaux, une douzaine de fraises mûres, une cuillerée à café de marasquin, demi-verre de cognac Curlier, une cuillerée à café de sirop de fraises, frapper fortement, passer, verser dans un verre vert C; remplir avec du champagne Henriot Sillery supérieur, une fraise, chalumeaux et servir.

Nᵒ 171 ## WHISKEY JULEP
#### Verre rouge B

Dans un verre rouge B, piler 3 ou 4 branches de menthe fraîche avec une cuillerée de sucre en poudre, puis 1 verre à liqueur de scotch whisky; remplir de scotch whisky, 1 verre à liqueur de chartreuse jaune, finir avec de l'eau, bien remuer, tremper dans du jus de citron une petite branche de menthe, l'ajuster au milieu du verre, chalumeaux, fruits selon la saison, 2 traits de bon rye whisky, saupoudrer le tout de sucre en poudre et servir.

# CINQUIÈME PARTIE

—◆◆—

# WINTER DRINKS

## BOISSONS D'HIVER, CHAUDES

et leurs

## PRÉPARATIONS

————◆✱◆————

# CINQUIÈME PARTIE

# BOISSONS D'HIVER

## CHAUDES

Les Boissons Américaines chaudes sont presqu'aussi originales que les autres glacées, toutes sont délicieuses et un grand nombre sont recommandées par nos plus éminents docteurs comme souveraines contre les plus forts rhumes et maladies des bronches.

Elles ne demandent aucun ustensile spécial et leur fabrication est d'une simplicité qui les met à la portée de tous.

En ce moment, en France, parmi les boissons les plus renommées, je citerai le Tom and Jerry qui remplace avantageusement les laits de poule de nos ancêtres et qui est d'une efficacité incontestable pour les estomacs délicats.

Le Port wine Négus est aussi très en vogue en Amérique dans les salons de la haute société et remplace pour beaucoup les punchs chauds et grogs de nos soirées mondaines.

Pour la préparation des Winter Drinks, il faut toujours avoir soin de passer de l'eau chaude dans les verres que vous devez employer, afin de les empêcher de se casser par la chaleur trop vive des boissons que vous y versez, et de toujours disssoudre le sucre dans l'eau avant d'y verser aucun alcool, afin d'en avoir plus promptement la dissolution.

Pour le service de quelques boissons, il sera bon de se munir de quelques porte-verres (page 113) de deux grandeurs, afin de les adapter aux verres B et C, pour préserver les doigts de la trop vive chaleur en buvant, et de toujours avoir quelques épices, clous de girofle, canelle, etc.

# USTENSILES POUR WINTER DRINKS
## BOISSONS CHAUDES

### Porte Verre Mazagran

Modèle uni, bord fort Pièce **7** »
   »   à jours   »   »   **7** »
   »   guilloché  »   »   **8** »

### Tasse Porcelaine

Petite . . . . . pièce  **3 fr. 25**
Grande. .    »   **4 fr.** »

| MÉTAL BLANC | | Avivé | Argenté |
|---|---|---|---|
| Contenance 1 verre pièce | | 13 » | 17 » |
| » 2 » | » | 16 » | 19 » |
| » 3 » | » | 19 » | 22 » |
| » 4 » | » | 22 » | 26 » |

### Porte-Épices

3 coquilles (intérieur doré)

Pièce. . . **35 fr.**

# BOISSONS CHAUDES, WINTER DRINKS

### N⁰ 172     AMERICAN GROG

VERRE B

Faire chauffer une cuillerée à bouche de sirop de gomme, moitié rhum vieux et eau, bien remuer, verser, 1 rond de citron dans lequel on passe 4 clous de girofle, porte-verre et servir.

### N⁰ 173     ALE FLIP (LAIT DE POULE A LA BIÈRE)

VERRE B

Faire chauffer demi-verre de (allsopp's) pale ale, mélanger à part 1 œuf avec une cuillerée à bouche de sucre poudre, saupoudrer de muscade, bien battre et verser tout doucement dans la bière par petite quantité en remuant vivement; puis verser d'un récipient dans un autre et lorsque se produit une mousse, verser dans votre verre, porte-verre et servir.

Cette boisson est délicieuse au commencement d'un rhume.

### N⁰ 174     BRANDY PUNCH (PUNCH AU COGNAC)

VERRE ROUGE E

Faire chauffer moitié fine champagne Curlier, moitié eau, une cuillerée de sucre poudre, verser et servir en flamme.

### N⁰ 175   BLUE BLAZES (FLAMMES BLEUES)
VERRE ROUGE E

Mélanger une cuillerée de sucre candie, une cuillerée de bon miel, finir moitié eau, moitié scotch whisky, faire chauffer et verser d'un récipient à un autre le liquide enflammé, afin de faire une longue traînée de flammes bleues et servir.

### N⁰ 176   CRITERION PORT NÉGUS
VERRE ROUGE E

Une cuillerée de sirop de gomme, finir avec du porto rouge Sandeman, faire chauffer, verser, une tranche de citron avec 3 clous de girofle et servir.

### N⁰ 177   GIN TODDY
VERRE C

Faire chauffer moitié gin, moitié eau, une cuillerée de sucre poudre, verser, porte-verre et servir.

### N⁰ 178   GIN CLING (CHAUD)
VERRE C

Faire chauffer moitié gin, une cuillerée de jus de citron, finir avec eau, une cuillerée de sucre poudre, verser, porte-verre et servir.

### N⁰ 179   OLD FASHIONED HOT GIN SLING
(GIN SLING A L'ANCIENNE MODE)
VERRE VERT E

Faire chauffer une cuillerée de sirop de gomme, moitié eau et moitié gin, gratter un peu de muscade, verser et servir.

Nᵒ 180          **ITALIEN FLIP**
VERRE C

Mélanger un jaune d'œuf bien frais, une cuillerée de sucre en poudre, demi-verre de fine champagne Curlier, finir avec du marsala, faire chauffer en battant fort verser, saupoudrer de muscade et servir.

Nᵒ 181          **JERSEY TODDY**
VERRE B

Faire chauffer une cuillerée de sucre en poudre, 1 bon verre d'eau-de-vie de cidre, demi-pomme cuite au four, finir avec de l'eau, verser, saupoudrer de muscade, porte-verre et servir.

Nᵒ 182          **KIRSCH PUNCH**
VERRE VERT E

Faire chauffer moitié kirsch vieux, moitié eau, une cuillerée de sucre en poudre, verser, servir avec flamme.

Nᵒ 183    **MILK PUNCH** (PUNCH AU LAIT CHAUD)
VERRE B

Faire chauffer demi-verre de bon lait, verser dans verre B rhum et cognac Curlier, en quantité égale, de la main droite, en agitant de la main gauche, saupoudrer de muscade, porte-verre et servir.

Nᵒ 184          **RUM PUNCH**
VERRE ROUGE E

Faire chauffer rhum vieux et eau en quantité égale, une cuillerée de sucre poudre, verser et servir.

### N° 185     RUM FLIP (CHAUD)
#### VERRE B

Faire chauffer demi-verre de pâle ale (allsopp's), mélanger à part 1 œuf bien frais, 1 verre à liqueur de bon rhum, saupoudrer de muscade et de gingembre, bien battre et faire chauffer doucement; ensuite, mélanger en versant d'un récipient dans un autre et servir lorsqu'il y a une mousse.

### N° 185     SANDEMAN'S PORT NÉGUS
#### VERRE ROUGE E

Faire chauffer une cuillerée de sirop de gomme, demi-verre à liqueur de cognac, finir avec du porto rouge Sandeman, verser, une tranche d'orange, 3 clous de girofle et servir.

### N° 187     PORT SANGAREE (CHAUD)
#### VERRE C

Faire chauffer moitié eau et porto rouge Sandeman, une cuillerée de sucre poudre, saupoudrer de muscade, verser, porte-verre et servir.

### N° 188     PUNCH CUSENIER SEC
#### VERRE E

Demi-verre de punch Cusenier, eau, demi-verre à liqueur de rhum, une cuillerée de sirop de gomme, faire chauffer et servir

### N⁰ 189     PUNCH DU 69ᴱ RÉGIMENT
#### Verre C

Faire chauffer demi-verre à liqueur d'irish whisky, demi-verre à liqueur de scotch whisky, une cuillerée en poudre, 3 traits de jus de citron, finir avec de l'eau, verser, une tranche de citron, porte-verre et servir.


### N⁰ 190     SLEEPER (DORMEUR)
#### Verre rouge E

Faire chauffer 1 jaune d'œuf bien frais, une cuillerée de jus de citron, une cuillerée de sucre en poudre, 2 clous de girofle, 1 morceau de canelle, finir avec rhum et eau, verser, porte-verre et servir.


### N⁰ 191     SHERRY SANGAREE (CHAUD)
#### Verre C

Faire chauffer moitié eau et sherry Sandeman, saupoudrer de muscade, verser, porte-verre et servir.


### N⁰ 192     TOM AND JERRY
#### Tasse

Faire bouillir de l'eau. Dans une tasse à Tom and Jerry, délayer un jaune d'œuf bien frais avec une cuillerée de sucre en poudre, verser de l'eau bouillante aux 3/4 de la tasse, finir avec rhum et cognac Curlier en quantité égale et mélanger en changeant plusieurs fois de la tasse dans un récipient bien chaud, afin de ne pas refroidir et servir avec toute la mousse en saupoudrant de muscade.

Maison fondée
en 1876

# 11, Rue Taitbout, Paris

Anc' : 17, Rue de Choiseul

CINQ MÉDAILLES D'OR
TROIS MÉDAILLES VERMEIL & ARGENT
aux Expositions Universelles & Internationales

# Emile Duvoye

## Graveur-Imprimeur

## SPÉCIALITÉ DE MENUS ARTISTIQUES

Fournisseur des premières Maisons de Paris

BRASSERIES, CAFÉS, HOTELS, RESTAURANTS, ETC. ETC.

Téléphone 149-24

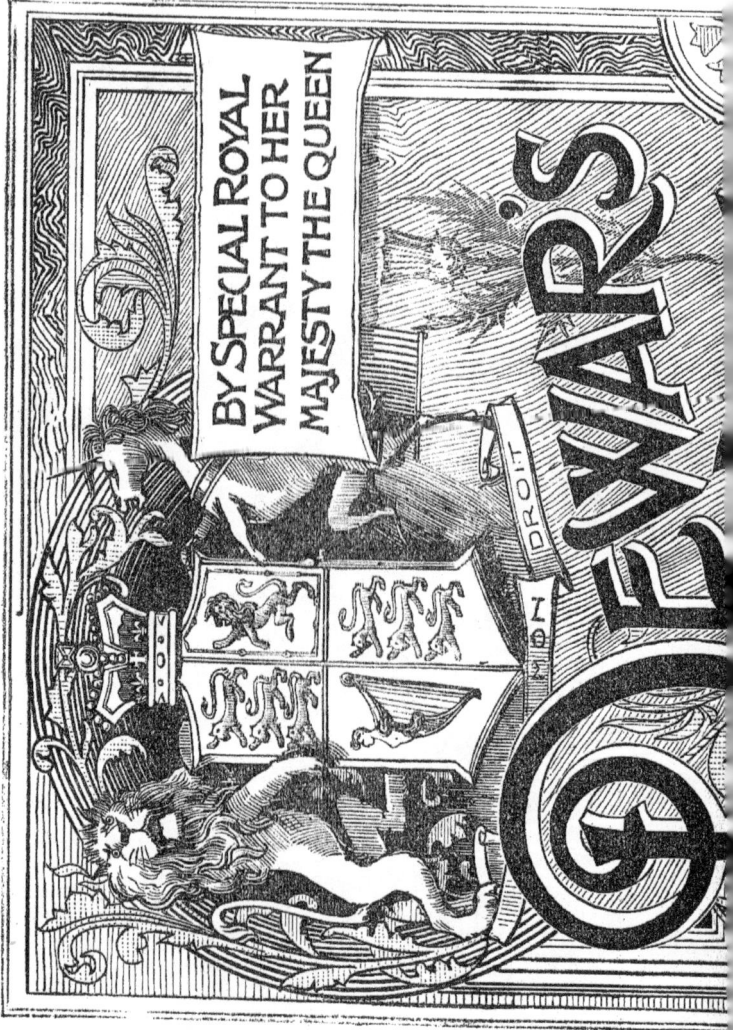

Perth Whisky

25 Gold & Prize Medals Awarded

John Dewar & Sons Ltd
DISTILLERS
ALSO
PERTH N.B. & LONDON
MANCHESTER BRISTOL & SYDNEY

Cinq Médailles d'Or, Trois Médailles Vermeil et Argent
aux Expositions Universelles et Internationales

Gravure & Impressions en Taille-Douce
Typographie

EMILE DUVOYE

Graveur

Paris

LITHOGRAPHIE

11 Rue Taitbout

ANC᭼ 17 RUE DE CHOISEUL

FACTURES, TÊTES DE LETTRES, ENVELOPPES
CARTES D'ADRESSE, CARTES D'INVITATION, CARTES D'ENVOI

BILLETS DE MARIAGE ET NAISSANCE

GRAVURE EN CREUX & EN RELIEF
Armoiries, Cachets, Médailles, Vaisselle

ACTIONS, CHÈQUES, MANDATS, TIMBRES-POSTE

Spécialité de Cartes de Visite gravrées sur cuivre
depuis **3.50** le cent

SANS FRAIS DE GRAVURE

**TÉLÉPHONE 149-24.**

**N⁰ 193**  ## WHISKEY PUNCH CHAUD
VERRE ROUGE E

Faire chauffer moitié whisky (scotch ou irish) et eau, une cuillerée de sucre en poudre, verser et servir en flammes.

**N⁰ 194**  ## WHISKEY FLIP (CHAUD)
VERRE C

Délayer un jaune d'œuf bien frais avec une cuillerée de sucre en poudre, finir avec scotch whisky et eau, faire chauffer, verser, saupoudrer de muscade et servir.

**N⁰ 195**  ## WHISKEY SLING (CHAUD)
VERRE C

Faire chauffer en quantité égale irish ou scotch whisky avec de l'eau, une cuillerée de sucre poudre, verser, saupoudrer de muscade, couper et presser 2 longs zestes de citron et servir.

**N⁰ 196**  ## WHISKEY TODDY
VERRE C

Faire chauffer moitié gin, moitié eau, une cuillerée de sucre en poudre et sèrvir sans citron verre C, avec porte verre.

# SIXIÈME PARTIE

---

# PUNCHS

pour

## SOCIÉTÉS & RÉUNIONS

et leurs

## PRÉPARATIONS

---

# SIXIÈME PARTIE

## 𝕻𝖚𝖓𝖈𝖍𝖘 𝖕𝖔𝖚𝖗 𝕾𝖔𝖈𝖎é𝖙é𝖘 & 𝕽é𝖚𝖓𝖎𝖔𝖓𝖘

J'ai cru devoir ne pas finir mon manuel d'American Drinks, sans ajouter quelques recettes de punchs chauds et froids pour réunions et sociétés, avec les quantités pour un nombre déterminé de personnes, qu'il sera facile d'augmenter ou de diminuer, selon le nombre des convives.

Pour les punchs chauds, il sera préférable de les préparer dans des bassines de terre très épaisse et de ne les conserver absolument que pour cet usage.

Pour les punchs froids, de grands bols suffiront pour faire n'importe quelle boisson.

Toujours avoir soin de mettre des fruits en profusion en servant les punchs froids, ainsi que des chalumeaux que l'on servira à part.

# BOL & PORTE-CUILLÈRES

pour le

# SERVICE DES PUNCHS POUR SOCIÉTÉS

**Porte-Cuillères**...... Pièce **45** fr.

**Bol à Citrons ou Oranges**
Argenté............... Pièce **40** fr.

### Nᵒ 197 PUNCH SANDEMAN AU XÉRÈS

**POUR 2 PERSONNES**

Demi-bouteille de sherry Sandeman, 2 cuillerées à bouche de sucre poudre, une orange coupée en tranches minces, 3 tranches de citron, bien glacer et mélanger, fruits de la saison, servir dans verre B avec chalumeaux.

### Nᵒ 198 PUNCH DE TOUS LES JOURS

**POUR 2 PERSONNES**

Glace pilée, 1 verre à madère de cognac Curlier, demi-verre à madère de vin de Bordeaux, 1 verre à liqueur d'absinthe blanche, une cuillerée à bouche de sucre poudre, 2 traits de sirop de gomme, finir avec eau fraîche, bien mélanger et servir dans verre C.

### Nᵒ 199 PUNCH AU CIDRE

**POUR 10 PERSONNES**

Verser un quart de litre de sherry Sandeman doux sur une douzaine de zestes de citron, 125 grammes de sucre en poudre, saupoudrer de muscade, une bouteille de cidre, bien mélanger, placer le bol sur la glace et ajouter au moment de servir un verre de fine champagne Curlier et quelques tranches de pelures de concombre et servir dans verre C.

### Nᵒ 200 PUNCH IMPÉRIAL FRANÇAIS

**POUR 10 PERSONNES**

Une bouteille de vin rouge, une bouteille de soda water, 4 cuillerées à bouche de sucre poudre, demi-cuillerée à café de muscade en poudre, glace en morceaux, 3 pelures de concombre, bien mélanger et servir dans verre C.

# CHAMPAGNE AYALA

*Maison fondée à AY en* **1853**

## GRANDS VINS SECS

### GOUT ANGLAIS

**8** francs **50** la Bouteille

## GRANDS VINS DEMI-SECS OU DOUX

### GOUT FRANÇAIS

**7** francs **50** la Bouteille

**CH. HEINE,** *Agent pour la France,*

5, rue du Faubourg-Saint-Honoré

**PARIS**

# PORTO SANDEMAN

*Maison fondée à OPORTO en* **1790**

## MÉDAILLES D'OR

## AUX EXPOSITIONS DE PARIS 1878 et 1889

Maison à **Oporto** : SANDEMAN et Cº.
  — **Jerez de la Frontª** : SANDEMAN, BUCK et Cº.
  — **Lisbonne** : SANDEMAN BROTHERS.
  — **Londres** : Geo. G. SANDEMAN, SONS et Cº.

**CH. HEINE,** *Agent pour la Belgique et la France,*

5, rue du Faubourg-Saint-Honoré

**PARIS**

### Nᵒ 201     PUNCH DE L'INDÉPENDANCE
#### POUR 12 PERSONNES

Une bouteille de rye whisky, 1/4 litre de rhum Jamaïque, 1 litre d'eau pure, couper 6 citrons en tranches minces, 1 ananas coupé en tranches, sucrer au goût, glacer et servir verre C.

### Nᵒ 202     PUNCH ROYAL
#### POUR 15 PERSONNES

Dans un grand bol, presser le jus de 5 citrons, 2 oranges bien douces, dissoudre 250 grammes de sucre poudre, ensuite déposer la pelure d'une orange finement épluchée, verser doucement le blanc de 6 œufs bien battus; verser une bouteille de champagne Henriot sec, demi-bouteille de rhum Jamaïque, bien mélanger, décorer avec des fruits de la saison, mettre le bol dans une glacière et servir une heure après.

### Nᵒ 203     PUNCH AU CHAMPAGNE
#### POUR 15 PERSONNES

Une bouteille de bordeaux rouge, 1/4 sucre en poudre, une orange coupée en tranches, jus d'un citron, 4 tranches d'ananas, 1 verre à liqueur de sirop de framboises, bien remuer, fruits de la saison, verser 2 bouteilles de champagne Henriot Silver label et servir dans des verres à champagne C.

### Nᵒ 204     PUNCH DU CRITERION
#### POUR 15 PERSONNES

Quart sucre en poudre, une bouteille de fine champagne Curlier, une bouteille de rhum, une bouteille d'eau pure, 1/4 de litre de curaçao, jus de 4 citrons, mélanger avec de gros morceaux de glace, fruits de la saison et servir dans des verres à champagne C.

## Nᵒ 205     LE PUNCH DE L'EUROPE
### POUR 15 PERSONNES

Quart de litre de sirop de framboises, 125 grammes de sucre poudre, 1 litre d'eau pure, 1 litre et demi de cognac Curlier, 1 citron coupé en tranches minces, demi-orange coupée, 6 tranches d'ananas, remplir avec glace pilée, orner avec fruits, oranges, etc., servir dans verre C, chalumeaux.

## Nᵒ 206     LE PUNCH DE FEU M. TOUPINEL
### POUR 20 PERSONNES

6 citrons en tranches minces, 2 bouteilles de rhum, 2 bouteilles de cognac Curlier, 500 grammes de sucre en poudre, 2 litres et demi d'eau pure, demi-litre de lait bouilli.

Faire tremper les citrons dans le cognac et le rhum pendant vingt-quatre heures; ensuite ajouter le sucre, l'eau et le lait et lorsque c'est bien mélangé, passer au clair. Ce punch peut être mis en bouteille et employé chaud ou froid.

## Nᵒ 207     PUNCH A L'ANANAS
### POUR 20 PERSONNES

4 bouteilles de champagne Henriot sec, 1/4 de litre de fine champagne Curlier, 1/4 de litre de rhum Jamaïque, 1 verre à madère de curaçao, jus de 4 citrons, 4 ananas coupés en tranches, sucrer au goût avec du sucre poudre.

Mettre les ananas coupés dans un grand bol, saupoudrer de sucre poudre, et lorsque le sucre est complètement dissous dans l'ananas, mettre tout le reste excepté le champagne et laisser le bol dans une glacière pendant une heure environ; ajouter ensuite le champagne avec un gros morceau de glace dans le milieu et orner avec fruits de la saison et tranches d'oranges, servir dans des verres C.

| N° 208 | # PUNCH A L'ORANGE |
|---|---|

**POUR 20 PERSONNES**

Presser 4 oranges, pelures d'une orange, 500 grammes de sucre en morceaux, 1 litre d'eau bouillante, laisser infuser une heure, ajouter un demi-litre de pale ale, demi-litre de cognac Curlier, verser encore un peu d'eau bouillante et parfumer avec du noyau, mettre dans une glacière, verser ensuite et servir dans des verres C.

On peut faire un punch au citron de la même manière en mettant des citrons au lieu d'oranges.

| N° 209 | # PUNCH DE LA MONTAGNE |
|---|---|

**POUR 20 PERSONNES**

5 bouteilles de champagne Jules Mumm, demi-bouteille de rhum Jamaïque, 1/4 litre de marasquin, 6 citrons coupés en tranches, sucrer au goût; bien mélanger le tout, placer au milieu du bol un bloc de glace, orner avec oranges, citrons, cerises à l'eau-de-vie, sucre candie, etc., et servir.

Voilà un délicieux punch pour fêter la nouvelle année!

### N° 210

# PUNCH DE LA GARDE NATIONALE DE NEW-YORK
## (LE NATIONAL GUARD N. Y. PUNCH)

**POUR 30 PERSONNES**

3 bouteilles de champagne Jules Mumm, une bouteille de sherry Sandeman sec, une bouteille de fine champagne Curlier, une bouteille de Sauternes (Château Peyron), un ananas coupé en tranches minces, 4 citrons coupés en tranches minces, sucrer au goût, bien mélanger avec de gros morceaux de glace et servir immédiatement.

### Nᵒ 211    PUNCH DE COLOMBIE

**POUR 30 PERSONNES**

3 bouteilles de champagne Henriot sec, une bouteille de curaçao, une bouteille de cognac Curlier, demi-bouteille de rhum Jamaïque, 2 bouteilles de madère Sandeman, 2 bouteilles de soda water, 1 kilo de raisins secs; ajouter des oranges, citrons, sucre candie, une petite infusion de thé vert; laisser dans une glacière pendant deux heures, bien mélanger, glace et servir dans verre B.

### Nᵒ 212    PUNCH NEC PLUS ULTRA

**POUR 60 PERSONNES**

6 bouteilles de bordeaux rouge, 6 bouteilles de soda water, une bouteille de fine champagne Curlier, une bouteille de sherry Sandeman, demi-litre d'infusion de thé vert, jus de 3 citrons, demi-ananas coupé en tous petits morceaux, sucrer au goût; bien mélanger, laisser reposer, passer et mettre en litres; garder un mois avant de servir.

### Nᵒ 213    PUNCH EUGÈNE BARDIOT ESQ.

**POUR 80 PERSONNES**

1 kilo de sucre poudre, 6 bouteilles de soda water, 6 bouteilles de champagne Henriot, 2 bouteilles de bordeaux rouge, 4 bouteilles de vin du Rhin, une bouteille de cognac Curlier, 4 bouteilles d'eau filtrée, couper en tranches minces 3 citrons, 1 ananas, 4 oranges; bien mélanger, glace en morceaux et servir dans verre B avec fruits de la saison et chalumeaux.

## N⁰ 214     LOUIS' PUNCH CHAUD

**POUR 12 PERSONNES**

Quart de litre d'infusion de thé vert, demi-litre de rhum Jamaïque, demi-litre de cognac Curlier, 1 verre à liqueur de curaçao, jus de 2 citrons, sucrer au goût, 125 grammes de gelée de pieds de veau, faire chauffer et servir verre C.

Boire le plus chaud possible.

## N⁰ 215     PUNCH CHAUD AU COGNAC

**POUR 15 PERSONNES**

Demi-litre de rhum Jamaïque, demi-litre de cognac Curlier, 500 grammes de sucre en morceaux, 4 citrons coupés en tranches, 1 litre d'eau pure, une cuillerée à café de muscade en poudre; bien faire chauffer, mélanger et servir dans verre C, porte-verre.

# RECIPE INDEX

## C

## H

## I

## J

# K

# L

# M

## Q

## R

S

---

# ABOUT THE AUTHOR

Charles Vexenat's love affair with liquid started when he was only six years old, mixing syrups and lemonade behind the bar at his grandparents' brasserie in Dijon.

When he moved to London in 2000 to learn English he naturally gravitated to the bar industry to earn his keep. Starting as a kitchen porter and food runner, he worked his way up through the business learning from an international array of the industry's best mentors.

He has since worked in London's top bars: Hush, Eagle Bar Diner, Che, Lab, La Floridita, and Lonsdale as well as at Tres Agaves in San Francisco plus PDT and Death & Company in New York. He also collaborates on regular basis with top bar consultants involving himself from concept through to training and design.

His passion for cocktail books started at the outset of his career and has kept growing to the present day. He has won many bartending competitions, and was twice awarded 2007 Best Bartender in UK. He has also visited and worked in different distilleries around the world, notably in Mexico.

Charles currently freelances as a trainer and bar consultant, delivering inspiring training sessions and creating drinks around the world.

www.ingramcontent.com/pod-product-compliance
Lightning Source LLC
Chambersburg PA
CBHW020507100426
42813CB00030B/3152/J